The Revolution

in Statecraft

Books of related interest in
Duke Press Policy Studies

Henry S. Bradsher, *Afghanistan and the Soviet Union*

Dan Caldwell, ed., *Henry Kissinger: His Personality and Policies*

Ivan Volgyes, *The Political Reliability of the Warsaw Pact Armies: The Southern Tier*

Robert Weller and Scott Guggenheim, eds., *Power and Protest in the Countryside: Studies in Rural Unrest*

Andrew M. Scott

The Revolution
in Statecraft

Intervention in an Age

of Interdependence

Duke Press Policy Studies Paperbacks

Durham, N.C.   1982

Chapter VII is reprinted by permission of New York University Press from *Czechoslovakia: Intervention and Impact*, edited by I. William Zartman. Copyright © 1970 by New York University Press. Chapter VIII is published by permission of the *Journal of International Affairs* and the Trustees of Columbia University in the City of New York.

Library of Congress Cataloging in Publication Data

Scott, Andrew MacKay.
   The revolution in statecraft.

   (Duke Press policy studies paperbacks)
   Expanded ed. of author's 1965 work of same title.
   Includes index.
   1. International relations.   2. World politics.   I. Title.   II. Series.
JX1395.S35   1982   327.1   82-9768
ISBN 0-8223-0494-5 (pbk.)   AACR2

Contents

Publisher's Foreword   vii

Introduction   xi

I. World Politics and Informal Penetration   3

II. Informal Attack: The Nazi and Soviet
    Experience   30

III. The Revolution in American Statecraft   69

IV. Disloyalty, Ideology, and Informal Access   113

V. International Organizations and Informal
    Penetration   140

VI. Informal Penetration and the Nation-State
    System   156

VII. Military Intervention by the Great Powers: The
    Rules of the Game   177

VIII. Nonintervention and Conditional
    Intervention   198

Index   208

Publisher's Foreword

In the rapidly moving world of international politics, a book is often out-of-date within a year or two and, sometimes, indeed, before it even reaches the hands of readers. It was a pleasure therefore to encounter a book written in the early 1960s and published in 1965 that remains fresh and full of insights relevant to the 1980s.

When Andrew Scott's *The Revolution In Statecraft*: *Informal Penetration* was issued in that year by Random House, the term "interdependence" had not come into common use and the important reality that it pointed to was not yet widely recognized. His book was one of the first to perceive that changing reality and to look beneath its surface. Because that look was so penetrating his book can withstand the challenge of being reissued seventeen years later.

The author perceived one of the most important aspects of interdependence—the increase in the porosity of national borders—and asked a series of questions about that development.

— What are the central characteristics of the change?
— Can we trace its origins?
— What are its implications for the foreign policy practices of nations?
— What are its implications for ideological change and how are the loyalties of individuals likely to be affected?

— What does it mean for the operation of international organizations and for their future?

— What will be its overall impact on the functioning of the nation-state system?

The book is presented as it first appeared, save that the author has written a new Introduction and has added two chapters, VII and VIII, which round out his discussion of intervention and add richness to his analysis of the implications of permeability.

Chapter VII, "Military Intervention by the Great Powers: The Rules of the Game," is a paper prepared for delivery at a conference at New York University in December, 1968 following the Soviet invasion of Czechoslovakia; this paper was later published in *Czechoslovakia: Intervention and Impact*, ed. I. William Zartman (New York: New York University Press, 1970). It discusses the nature of modern spheres of influence, giving bite and substance to that concept, and shows how military intervention by a superpower, and the reaction of the other to it, will be affected by the existence of such spheres. This chapter illuminates the interventionary behavior of both the United States and the Soviet Union, when it comes to military operations, and makes extremely interesting reading in the light of the events in Poland in late 1981 and early 1982.

Chapter VIII, "Nonintervention and Conditional Intervention," appeared in the *Journal of International Affairs*, 22 (1968): 208-216. It asks what happens to the concept of "nonintervention" in an era in which governments routinely intervene in the affairs of other societies. The newer techniques of intervention and informal penetration—economic aid, technical assistance, cultural exchange programs, information programs, military aid, military training missions, arms sales, export licensing arrangements, and so on—constitute the very means by which powerful nations exercise leadership, provide assistance, and seek to shape events. Furthermore, governments of recipient nations, far from resenting such intervention, may request it and compete with one another to see which will get the most of it.

The Duke University Press is pleased to have the opportunity to make this important study, now out of print for some years and hard to find, available once again.

Andrew M. Scott is Professor of Political Science at the University of North Carolina—Chapel Hill. He received his Ph.D. from Harvard University in 1950 and worked in economic aid and intelligence agencies in Washington for some years.

His writing on international affairs includes *The Anatomy of Communism* (1951), *Simulation and National Development (1966), The Functioning of the International Political System* (1967), *Insurgency* (1970), and, most recently, *The Dynamics of Interdependence* (1982).

Introduction

Through most of the lifetime of the nation-state system national borders have been relatively impervious to penetration by agents of another society, save in the case of espionage or armed aggression. Relations between nations were predominantly of a formal, government-to-government nature. It could hardly have been otherwise.

Since World War I there has been a striking increase in the porosity of national borders, an increase that has been both effect and cause. Rapid advances in technology have contributed to this change and it, in turn, created conditions which allowed new forms of statecraft to come into existence; these, in their turn, contributed to further increases in porosity.

The statecraft practiced by nations usually fits the conditions of the time fairly well. It is not surprising therefore that, in the earlier world of hard-shell nations, relations were formal. As those conditions changed however, and borders became more permeable, one would expect to see changes in the techniques of statecraft. Such has been the case. Techniques have emerged that provide a government with direct access to the people and processes of another society. Formal relations continue, of course, but they have come to be supplemented by the techniques of informal penetration, and this addition has radically altered the practice of statecraft among nations.

In the case of the United States, these techniques have included economic aid, technical assistance, military aid, military advisory and training operations, support for insurgent or counterinsurgent operations, cultural exchange programs, a range of information activities including the use of international radio, the Peace Corps, and the various covert operations of the Central Intelligence Agency. Such activities now absorb more funds and occupy more people than do the traditional, formal techniques of diplomacy. It was the use of such techniques of informal penetration that gave the Cold War its distinctive cast.

On the international scene today it would be hard to find a completely "closed" system (one that does not exchange inputs or outputs with its environment) or a completely "open" system (one in which inputs flow without hindrance from the environment into a system and outputs flow freely from the sytem into the environment). Nevertheless one might think of "open" and "closed" systems as ideal types and imagine them at the extreme ends of a continuum. Any given nation can then be located somewhere along that continuum depending on its degree of openness. If national societies had been located along such a continuum in 1914 and were so located again today, a great many of them would be seen to have migrated from points near the "closed" end to locations much nearer the "open" end.

Any development that affects the workings of individual nation-states in a significant way, such as the growth in porosity or openness, must, when aggregated for a multitude of such states, have consequences for the system as a whole. What are some of those consequences? What does it mean for the global system that it is composed of relatively "open" subsystems and that the trend in that direction seems to be continuing? While the increase in porosity has revolutionized the techniques of statecraft, its consequences by no means stop there. In an international system composed of open subsystems there will be a great deal of interaction, for porosity at the national level and interaction and interdependence at the level of the global system are little more than different aspects of the same thing.

The present is often spoken of as an era of inter-dependence. Many of the characteristics associated with interdependence are related, directly or indirectly, to this increasing permeability. For example, policy actions of major nations now ramify widely through the entire inter-active system and, conversely, what happens in that system will often have a powerful impact within individual nations. As national economies have become more open and less self-contained a progressively more tightly-knit global economy has emerged. Economists must now con-cern themselves not only with inflation, employment, recession, debt, and balance of payments problems at the national level but also with the system-wide problems that such things create or reflect.

The permeability of national borders to modern weapons has important implications for the global system and so does the inability of national borders to contain the consequences of an attack. Radioactive clouds are no respecters of national boundaries. Similarly, borders rarely contain the consequences of the environmental practices of national societies. One thinks of atmospheric pollution and acid rain, pollution of the oceans, inadver-tent weather change and the CO_2 problem, and so on. The permeability of national borders to the movement of persons has, as one of its results, the emergence of an international refugee problem.

As the borders of an individual nation become more porous the flow of cultural items across them is apt to increase. Multiply that result for over 150 nations and what emerges is a global system in which diffusion pro-cesses are more rapid and pervasive than ever before in history. Individuals quickly learn to want the kinds of goods and services available in other societies—French wines, Japanese cars and color television sets, American-made jeans—and so consumables, in an astonishing vari-ety, now move across borders. Entertainment forms diffuse easily—records, films, television shows—as do many technologies, attitudes and ideas. Styles in dress and styles in political action spread with almost equal ease. Political kidnapping, airplane hijacking, and seizing hostages as a basis for making demands, all became internationally popular in the 1970s. Disease and pests also diffuse more easily since they can take advantage of international air travel and fast ocean freight.

Change is rarely cost-free. It is seldom possible to take the benefits of interdependence while leaving the costs behind. The diffusion of new technologies to developing societies is usually helpful in some respects and disruptive in others. So, too, at the global level. New technologies may be helpful in some respects, but they are turned loose on the world as quickly as they emerge and the world is left to cope with their unforeseen consequences as best it can. The rapid spread of nuclear technologies is a case in point and perhaps the spread of new communication technologies will be another. As floods of information become available there are bound to be new problems as well as new opportunities. For example, rapid communication may facilitate the speedy up-dating of stereotypes, which is presumably all to the good; but it may, just as easily, facilitate the spread of new passions and militantly intolerant new ideologies. The possibilities for international mass movements are sobering. The new technologies will also diffuse information about the misery in the world—wars, hunger, *coups*, assassinations, forced labor, crime, unemployment—and one can wonder how much vicarious misery and anxiety people can handle. Will that add new instabilities to the global system?

What will be the impact on custom of high rates of diffusion? Importation of "the new" is a powerful solvent of established ways of doing things, as has been dramatically demonstrated in a number of developing countries. After all, displacement of the old and the obsolescent must go hand-in-hand with the spread of the new. Since humankind, historically, has relied on custom to guide much of its behavior, what happens to the functioning of the global system as diffusion erodes customary patterns of behavior?

Since nation-states were the constituent elements as the nation-state system as it took shape after the Treaty of Westphalia in 1648, it is almost superfluous to note that they were well adapted to that world. They are much less at ease however in the permeable and interdependent world that has come into being during this century, and for reasons that are not hard to find. The growth of transnationalism and the declining efficacy of nation-states as problem solvers have gone together: both are aspects of the transformation of the global system. Permeability of national borders was a precondition for the emergence of a variety of transnational organizations such as multinational corporations, international nongovernmental organizations, and some international governmental organizations. As long as the world of hard-shell nation-states persisted they could not come into existence, and the fact that they are now so numerous and prominent is a measure of the extent to which the global system has been transformed by the emergence of national units that are more open.

The end is not yet in sight. Governments prefer that there be little outside influence on events within national borders yet transnational organizations are engaged in the internationalization of activities, issues, problems, and opinions. While the thrust of government is to limit and control the permeability of national borders, transnational organizations tend to see national borders as impediments to their easy operation. The logic of transnationalism would lead to a world in which borders became so porous and insubstantial as to have little significance. Nation-states, understandably, find it difficult to operate under conditions of porosity and increasing interdependence but transnational organizations take to those conditions like ducks to water; and why not, they evolved precisely in response to those conditions.

As a consequence of technological advance and an increase in porosity and interdependence, the global system that now exists is quite different from the system that existed before World War I.

— There are many more actors on the international scene than there were (multinational corporations, international governmental organizations, supranational organizations, sub-national groups such as guerilla and terrorist units, as well as new nations).

— With the web of global interaction becoming ever more tightly knit, fewer populations are left completely outside the flow of events.

— New forms of cooperation and conflict have emerged.

— With actors taking advantage of broad repertoires of actions, the amount of interaction in the global system is now much higher than it was. The number of actions taking place in a given unit of time has risen sharply, accelerating the tempo of events.

— Global problems have increased in number.

— Their scope has also tended to broaden, with local problems being increasingly replaced by regional problems and regional problems giving way to global problems.

— These problems are often intertwined with one another. Therefore actions taken to remedy one problem may well exacerbate other problems. (For example, policies designed to foster high rates of economic growth also tend to hasten resource depletion, promote global inflation, and speed the degradation of the environment).

— The acceleration of events, coupled with the increasing complexity and scope of the problems to be dealt with, means that problems now come in rapid succession, are harder to analyze, and are harder to deal with.

— Nation-states, including superpowers, therefore have trouble dealing with these problems.

The newer techniques of statecraft may have improved the capacity of individual nations to deal with one another bilaterally but they have done little to improve their capacity to deal with the emergent global problems associated with system transformation. Those problems are beyond the reach of individual nations and require a collective response. Will the nation-state system be capable of channelling and guiding the economic and other forces set loose in this era of interdependence? Looking ahead, one can see challenges on the horizon that, taken together, will be unprecedented, but no corresponding improvements in management capabilities are yet in sight.

These are issues which confront scholars and practitioners more urgently today than when this book was first published in 1965. I am pleased, therefore, that the Duke University Press has elected to re-issue it in order to give its argument a further hearing.

Andrew M. Scott
March 1982.

The Revolution

in Statecraft

CHAPTER I

World Politics
and Informal Penetration

Cold warfare has become the dominant mode of conflict among nations in the modern world, yet it is little understood. Few persons can give a satisfying answer to the question: What are the distinctive features of this type of conflict that make it unlike conflicts in preceding centuries?

The list of activities that would normally be placed in the Cold War category includes all of the following and many others: collaboration among the NATO powers; armament programs; economic aid; military aid; training of civilian and military officials of other nations; Voice of America broadcasts; organization of guerilla campaigns; activities of Communist parties and other Communist auxiliaries and front organizations; *coups d'état;* overseas information programs; cultural exchange programs; technical assistance; and subsidizing of political parties, newspapers, labor unions, and other organizations.

One thing that stands out clearly in this list is the contrast between the more traditional forms of activity —primarily diplomatic and military—and the newer forms. And it is in these newer forms that the special nature of cold warfare must be sought. What do these activities, seemingly so diverse—guerilla operations, cultural exchange, economic aid, and so on—have in common? This study will suggest that all of them are means by which the agents or instruments of one country gain access to the population (or parts of it) or processes of another country. This "informal access" or "informal penetration," as it will be called, is the central feature of cold warfare today.

Throughout the history of the nation-state system, relations between nations have been almost exclusively formal. A notable feature of the system has been the relative immunity of its component parts to planned interpenetration. Nations were set apart in space, and conflict and cooperation among them were conditioned by this separateness. Consequently, their relations were of a formal, government-to-government nature, carried on primarily by soldiers and diplomats. Only in wartime, and then only in a limited way, did one nation penetrate another or have access to its population. By their very nature, then, formal relations do not readily lend themselves to the purposeful initiation of social change in one society by the agents of another.

But, in this century, changes have taken place. Formal, government-to-government relations have been increasingly supplemented by *informal* relations, in which the agents or instruments of one country are able to reach inside the borders of another, with or without the knowledge and approval of the government of the second country.

Figure 1.1 depicts nations A, B, and C in a situation in which A is using traditional forms of external pressure against the other two.

This assumes an international system in which the nations operate as billiard balls, that is, they are assumed to be self-contained units moving in accordance with external pressures.

Figure 1.2 depicts the use of informal access, in which the influence of A reaches directly into B and C.

A more common situation would be one in which Nation A used formal pressure and informal access simul-

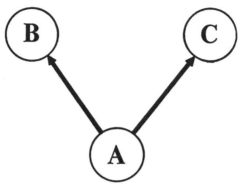

Figure 1.1

taneously against target Nations B and C, as depicted in Figure 1.3.

Hitherto, if Nation A wanted to move B along a certain course, its capacity to do so was limited by its ability to bring appropriate external pressure to bear on B. The very application of this pressure, however, might strengthen B in its decision to resist and unify its population around a policy of resistance. On the other hand, if A, in addition to exerting external pressure, were in a position to operate inside B and to influence public and official opinion, its position might be greatly strength-

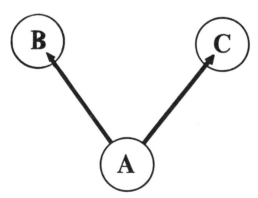

Figure 1.2

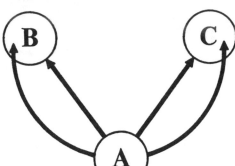

Figure 1.3

ened. Internal pressure would then supplement external pressure.

Informal techniques are as much instruments of foreign policy as formal ones. Each can be used in conjunction with the other, and, in combination, they have often proved deadly. Hitler was adept at using diplomatic pressure on a country in conjunction with the internal pressures generated by a dissident minority or Nazi-supported movement. The demands of the Sudeten German party against the Czechoslovak government, for example, were carefully coordinated with the official activities of the German government.

Informal penetration may be said to exist, then, when one country's agents or instruments come into contact with the people or processes of another country in an effort to achieve certain objectives. An exchange of diplomatic notes would not satisfy this definition, but an information program would. A blockade, an embargo, a trade-agreements act, or the freezing of a nation's assets would involve *formal,* government-to-government relations. Governmental exploitation of a cartel arrangement, on the other hand, would be a means of *informal* access. Furthermore, most, but not all, of the techniques of informal penetration require some face-to-face contact (a Voice of America broadcast is one example that does not). Personal contact, then, is a typical, but not a necessary, characteristic of informal access.

If informal access is the central feature of cold warfare today, it was also the distinctive feature of cold warfare yesterday. Cold warfare antedates the Cold War. It is a special type of conflict of which *the* Cold War is but one example. The latter is usually dated from 1946, but the *era* of cold warfare might better be dated from 1917, the year the Bolsheviks took power in Russia, or 1919, the year the Communist International was formed. Thus, although the term "Cold War" did not come into use until after the Second World War, this type of conflict existed between World Wars I and II. In studying the new modes of conflict, therefore, the analyst should begin his inquiry not with 1946 but a generation earlier.

Cold warfare during the interwar period was normally referred to by such terms as "Trojan horse tactics" or "fifth column activities," but the substance was the same. Yesterday's "fifth column" activity is today's "cold warfare," or "protracted conflict," or "new imperialism," and terminological differences should not be allowed to obscure the basic similarity. Indeed, the terms "Trojan horse" and "fifth column" are perhaps more suggestive of the nature of this form of conflict than is the term "cold warfare." By means of the hollow horse, a handful of Greeks penetrated the defenses of Troy and threw open the gates of the city at night to the returning Greek forces. "Fifth column" was first used in Spain at the beginning of October, 1936, when the rebel general, Emilio Mola, said that the Franco forces would launch four columns against Madrid but that the offensive would be begun by the fifth column already in the city. These examples emphasize the penetration of one camp by the agents of the other camp. Both terms are too limited, however, since they involve only war and armed insurrection. Informal access is, in fact, characteristic of a wide range of conflict techniques, many of which do not involve arms and violence.

The term "cold warfare" will, no doubt, remain in use, but it is, nevertheless, seriously inadequate. It draws the user into confusing cold warfare and the Cold War, and hence into the assumption that the era of informal penetration began with the Cold War. This is one of the reasons why the storehouse of experience gained by the Soviet Union and Nazi Germany between World Wars I and II has not been subjected to careful analysis. It has not been considered relevant to post-World War II problems. Moreover, use of the term "cold warfare" leads the user into dichotomous thinking. It encourages him to assume that the conflict possibilities are exhausted by the categories of Hot War and Cold War rather than to think in terms of a conflict continuum. Analysis is inhibited, therefore, rather than stimulated. In addition, the term "cold warfare" is singularly unsuggestive. It does not direct attention toward the vital importance of informal penetration. Finally, the term directs attention exclusively toward the *conflict* aspects of international politics. Yet the new forms of support that have been developed and the new forms of cooperation that have been devised are just as important to the understanding of contemporary international politics as are the new modes of conflict.

Informal penetration is a twentieth-century phenomenon or, more precisely, a post-World War I phenomenon. This is not to say, of course, that isolated examples of informal access do not extend back through history, for they assuredly do. Examples can be readily identified during times of revolutionary change, such as the French Revolution and the Wars of Religion. The development of the British Empire, and the diplomatic history of France, provide further examples. Americans might find an instance in the French penetration of North America by the use of Indian tribes. The affair of

Citizen Genet also comes to mind. In 1793, a time when France was at war with England and Spain, this eager individual arrived in the United States as minister plenipotentiary of the French Republic. He immediately fitted out privateers and recruited forces for the conquest of Florida, Louisiana, and Canada. Then, when these policies met with the opposition of President Washington, Citizen Genet sought to take the issue directly to the American people by organizing opposition to the government.

The existence of a wealth of historical examples must not be allowed to obscure the fact that there are important differences between informal penetration in the present and in the past. The achievement of historical perspective is of first importance, but the danger that often goes hand in hand with an attempt to achieve it is the tendency to overlook innovation. History provides a bottomless bag of facts, and, with a little groping, it is usually possible to demonstrate that anything that appears new is really old and has happened dozens of times elsewhere and been forgotten. Because it is so difficult to find anything that is totally new in *kind,* the historical approach makes it easy to overlook novelty when it takes the mundane form of changes in degree or a new combination of familiar factors. A number of factors taken together clearly distinguish twentieth-century informal penetration from what has gone before:

1. Informal access may characterize the relations of countries working together as well as of those in conflict.

2. It is used to achieve a variety of objectives ranging from *attack* at one end of the spectrum to *support* at the other.

3. Informal attack may be used as a prelude to military operations or as an adjunct to them. It may also be used as a substitute for military operations; in fact, in the present era of the Cold War, informal attack is more often used that way rather than in conjunction with military force.

4. A wide variety of techniques are used. They may be

violent or non-violent, covert or overt. A partial list would include technical assistance, economic aid, military aid, military training missions, cultural exchange programs, information and propaganda activities, the use of front groups, financial subsidy of various organizations, the use of economic warfare techniques, organization of guerilla warfare, sabotage, strikes and riots, establishment of militant party formations, and the organization of *coups d'état*.

5. These techniques are used against a variety of targets—nations; minorities; groups; parties.

6. Usually only diplomats and soldiers participate in formal governmental relations. But the cast of characters involved in informal relations is much more extensive— the labor organizer, economic aid adviser, military adviser, military training officers, guerilla or counterinsurgency instructors, newspapermen, information officers, CIA agents, foreign service officers, public administrators, public health advisers, engineers, businessmen, and scores of others. Because both the techniques of informal penetration and the targets against which they are used are diverse, personnel must also be varied.

7. Technology has been pressed into the service of informal access in a variety of ways, most notably, perhaps, in the field of electronic communications.

8. Objectives, targets, techniques, and personnel must be planned and coordinated if they are to be effective. Informal support and attack measures, therefore, tend to become highly complex, demanding the full-time attention of specialized personnel.

9. The growing complexity of informal operations, as well as the increased emphasis on them, has led to their institutionalization. Large organizations, massive budgets, extensive training programs, and all the paraphernalia of institutionalization are now involved.

10. Some penetration activities are overt and some covert. But, when a large organization is engaged in covert activities, its existence tends to become widely known. A nation may be able to maintain security with regard to particular operations, but the fact that it is engaged in the large-scale conduct of covert operations cannot remain a secret. Progressively larger numbers of per-

sons then come to regard the conduct of covert operations as a normal and continuing aspect of a nation's foreign affairs.

11. Informal access operations are playing an increasingly larger role in the foreign policy activities of the major nations. The greater the variety, depth, and geographical extent of a nation's interests, the greater is likely to be the variety, depth, and extent of its informal operations. Powers with global interests, such as the United States and the Soviet Union, regard virtually any area of the globe as a proper theater for their informal activities.

12. Some of the smaller nations are exploring the advantages of penetration activity, and it must be expected that their number will increase.

It may be useful to discuss the reasons why nations engage in informal penetration more than they once did. For one thing, public opinion is playing an increasingly important role in a great many nations. Even in countries where decision-making has not been democratized, the likes and dislikes, the wants and fears of the public are receiving increasing attention. In an earlier era, when decision-making tended to be the exclusive province of a monarch, a strong man, or a tiny elite, there was little point in trying to achieve access to the population as a whole since it was almost devoid of influence. Formal relations between governments were adequate. As public opinion began to carry more weight, however, the public became an important target for those outside the nation as well as those within. But access to it could be achieved only by means of informal penetration; hence the increased interest in this approach.

The development of sharp ideological cleavages also helps explain the growth of informal access. Not all techniques of informal penetration rely on ideological appeal, but, when ideological cleavages do exist, a much broader range of possibilities is opened up. It is safe to say that the large-scale practice of informal attack requires an ideological base that can be exploited.

Technology, too, has obviously been important in the development of informal operations. Communications and transportation are shrinking the globe and, at the same time, raising the level of interaction and interdependence among nations. The same forces that lead to greater interaction also foster increased interpenetration, since the opportunities for planned interpenetration are, to a considerable extent, a function of interaction. The world that was composed of relatively impermeable nation-states was based on a technology that offered limited means for communication and penetration. As technology advanced, the opportunities for penetration increased, and the day of the relatively impermeable nation-state passed.

Another contributing factor is the emergence of a large number of new nations in the years since the end of World War II. These nations have desired economic development but have been unable to achieve it without outside help. Such help, in the form of economic aid or technical assistance from other nations, almost invariably thrusts the granting nation into operational activities within the host country. The importance of this factor is made clear when it is realized that the United States alone has given aid to over one hundred countries.

Informal penetration was well established before the advent of nuclear weapons; hence, the development of the latter cannot be used to explain the emergence of the former. On the other hand, the development of super-weapons made full-scale warfare a less attractive instrument of national policy and thus led to an increased emphasis on limited modes of conflict, including informal attack. The growth of informal penetration is, therefore, associated with the development of super-weapons, even if it is not causally connected.

In his excellent and provocative book, *International Politics in the Atomic Age*,[1] John Herz has the following passage:

What is it, ultimately, that accounted for the peculiar unity, coherence, or compactness of the modern nation-state, setting it off from other nation-states as a separate unit and permitting us to characterize it as "independent," "sovereign," a "power"?

It would seem that this underlying something is to be found neither in the sphere of law, nor even in that of politics, but rather in the ultimate, and lowest, substratum where the state confronts us, in, as it were, its physical, corporeal capacity: as an expanse of territory, encircled for its identification and defense by tangible, military expressions of statehood, like fortifications and fortresses. In this lies what, for the lack of a better term, I shall refer to as the "impermeability," or "impenetrability," or simply the "territoriality" of the modern state.

In his later discussion, Professor Herz lists, in increasing order of importance, four factors he feels have served to break down the impenetrability of the modern state: the possibility of economic blockade; ideological-political penetration; air war; atomic war. Three of these factors—the first, third, and fourth—are available only when a nation is at war or is threatening war. The softening of the military hard shell around a nation is a revolutionary development, to be sure, but it is only one of the factors contributing to the progressive breakdown of the separateness of states. While Herz focuses on the factors associated with warfare, this study will emphasize the non-military factors that have tended to reduce the impenetrability of the modern state.

To say that one nation has informal access to another says nothing, in itself, about the use to which that access will be put. It may be used for purposes of attack, for purposes of support, or for purposes falling toward the middle of the spectrum that are neither the one nor the other. In terms of historical sequence, informal penetration was first exploited on a large scale in modern times for purposes of attack, as an examination of the activities of Nazi Germany and the Soviet Union in the following chapter will show. Informal support measures began to be elaborated somewhat later in response to both informal attack and traditional formal pressures.

Informal support must not be thought of as narrowly defensive, however. The range of possible responses is great, and a response may be developed that goes far beyond meeting the immediate challenge and alters the entire situation. Had there been no threat of Communism in Western Europe, the European Recovery Program (the Marshall Plan) would not have come when it did, nor on such a large scale. Once ERP was established, however, its ramifications soon passed beyond the limited objective of strengthening Europe economically so that it could resist Communism. Forces were set in motion that could not have been anticipated at the outset. Thus, the emergence of the Coal-Steel Community and the European Economic Community and the drive for common European political institutions would not have occurred without the Marshall Plan.

The field of cultural exchange, as noted earlier, also provides interesting examples of programs with consequences going quite beyond their original purposes. In much the same way, if the new nations had not become battlegrounds between the Communist and free worlds, programs of foreign aid and technical assistance would not have been undertaken at the present time and on the present scale. Yet the fact that these programs were undertaken is certain to lead to changes in these countries with the passage of time. An emergent nation that has received developmental aid for several years is not the same country it was at the beginning.

Even specialized techniques that are limited in their original concept may develop well beyond initial expectations. "Technical assistance" now is scarcely recognizable for what it was some years ago. Military assistance, too, has evolved in a variety of ways. Now the broad implications of information programs are apparent, as they were not when the programs were first developed. The local-currency counterparts of foreign aid have been put to uses never anticipated when this financial technique was originally conceived. The significance of a support technique, therefore, is rarely exhausted by pointing to the immediate challenge to which it was a response or to the limited purposes originally envisioned for it.

The concepts of "support" and "attack" are useful but they do not exhaust the possibilities. There is a middle range of activity that is both broad and important. The United States, for example, engages in programs abroad that cannot be characterized as involving either attack or support. It may operate an information program in a country in order to keep the attitudes of the populace friendly toward the United States with no thought of supporting or undermining the government or of modifying the society in a significant way. From the point of view of the country penetrated, this activity may appear legitimate and may seem neither helpful nor threatening.

It goes without saying that the concepts of "support" and "attack" are not precision instruments and that what one nation regards as support another may regard as attack. Measures that Americans would regard as supporting a friendly nation—training administrators and public health officials, engineering assistance, advice on economic planning—would probably be regarded by Soviet officials as efforts to subvert that nation, and vice versa. Observers might agree on the facts of what was taking place but not agree on the interpretation of those facts. The difficulty arises because the same act may be regarded as an example of attack or as an example of support depending upon the motivations and perceptions of the penetrating nation and the target nation.

If both the target nation and the penetrating nation feel that the target is being attacked, then it probably is being attacked. Or if both agree that the penetration represents support, it may be safely characterized as such. The more complicated situations arise when the two nations do not agree. A penetrating nation may have no purpose other than to help a target nation, yet the latter may attribute ulterior motives to it. Conversely, the penetrating nation may have sinister purposes that are not perceived by the target, or host, nation. For example, the commercial activities of a number of Eastern European and Latin American nations were intricately tied in with Hitler's Germany for some time before persons in those nations realized what had happened. And during the period 1936-39, when Nazi penetration of France was at its height, the French could not agree on whether a problem of Nazi penetration existed. Similarly in the 1930's, when Soviet penetration of American labor, cultural, and governmental affairs was extensive, many Americans could not agree that penetration had occurred or, if it had, that it was injurious.

How a target nation evaluates a given example of penetration may be deeply influenced by its estimate of the purposes of the penetrating nation. If it feels that the penetrating nation is basically friendly, it may be more tolerant of its access than it would be of that of another country. Of course, even if it understood that the motivation behind the penetration was thoroughly beneficent, it might be troubled by the cumulative effect of this penetration. One can fear bondage to one's friends as well as to one's enemies.

The relation of covert operations to informal penetration also needs clarification. There has been a marked increase in covert activities in recent decades, but covert activities and informal penetration are not the same thing since informal access may involve either covert or overt activities. For example, it may make a difference tactically whether the United States operates an information program through the United States Information Agency in a country (overt) or whether it engages in covert propaganda activities, but both programs are types of informal penetration. It may also make a difference tactically whether the United States Army trains guerillas in South Vietnam (overt) or whether it hires "volunteers" to do it (covert), but, here again, both programs would involve informal access. Although the overt/covert question may be of considerable operating importance, it does not involve significant changes in the structure and functioning of the nation-state system. The development of interpenetration on a large scale is, therefore, vastly more important than the question of whether governments officially acknowledge their informal involvement.

Five main types of informal access may be distinguished:

(1) informal governmental access;
(2) quasi-governmental access;
(3) non-governmental access;
(4) informal access by an international organization;
(5) informal access by a nation through the medium of an international organization.

Governmental access is achieved by agents of a governmental organization, such as the United States Information Agency, the State Department, the Agency for International Development (AID), the Defense Department, the Central Intelligence Agency, or the Department of Agriculture. Quasi-governmental access, the second of these categories, includes the activities of individuals abroad who are not formal agents of a government but have some special connection with it. The activities of some journalists and scholars or representatives of companies, such as United Fruit or Aramco, whose operations may occasionally have an almost governmental character, fit into this category. The third type, non-governmental access, includes the activities of missionaries, tourists, students, teachers, journalists, researchers, engineers, businessmen, and the like. Next, an international organization may gain informal access to the people or processes of a nation by virtue of its operations there. Finally, one country, through its position in an international organization, can gain access to others. For example, the predominant position of the United States in an international organization may allow it to influence that organization's policy and thereby wield an informal influence over the people and processes of other countries.

For most purposes these categories are serviceable enough, although there is, of course, overlap, and some examples of informal access are hard to classify. The Alliance for Progress, for example, presupposes a large volume of private investment in Latin America. It therefore becomes a part of the government's policy to stimulate such investment by means of favorable tax treatment of foreign earnings, generous depreciation allowances, and insurance against the expropriation of profits. The funds involved are private, not governmental; they are invested for profit and are privately administered. This suggests that the access deriving from this activity should be classified as non-governmental. On the other hand, by taking sufficiently strong steps, a government can virtually guarantee that private investment will be forthcoming. The government is then subsidizing the private investor, and this subsidy will certainly affect the line of development of the economy concerned. And, in that sense, it may ultimately have political consequences. This does not make the firms investing in Latin America agents of the United States government, but it does suggest that quasi-governmental access is involved. However, a question of this kind can arise only in connection with an economy that possesses a private sector. Soviet investment abroad, for example, is automatically governmental. And so is Soviet purchasing abroad through AMTORG (American Trading Organization) even though it provides informal access to the country in which the buying is done.

An instrument of access may be put to different uses. If, in addition to subsidizing firms investing abroad, a successful effort was made by the government to use those firms for purposes of propaganda and subversion, governmental access would clearly be involved. Virtually any commercial exchange or transaction reaching across national boundaries can be made to provide a form of governmental access. The development of foreign subsidiaries, establishment of branch plants abroad, negotiation of private loans or patent agreements, purchase or sale of raw materials or finished goods—any or all—may be exploited for governmental purposes under some conditions. German business concerns, for example, were involved in an intricate series of cartel arrangements prior to 1933. When these instruments began to be purposely exploited by the German government for political, military, and economic ends, however, they became instruments of governmental access. The same sort of convertible entree can exist in fields other than the economic. For example, a great many persons of German background lived abroad before the coming of Hitler and maintained contact with relatives and friends in Germany. By the systematic exploitation of these contacts, Hitler converted them from a non-governmental to a governmental form of access.

The fact that a program has a formal aspect does not prevent it from being essentially informal. Every information program, economic aid program, or cultural exchange program will have a formal aspect, since the mission is in the host country pursuant to a formal treaty. The essential criterion is not the formal element but the fact that the arrangement provides the penetrating nation with informal access to the host nation. Whether the program is formally endorsed by the host government, conducted with the knowledge of the host government but without its formal approval, or undertaken without the knowledge of the host government is not relevant from this point of view.

The choice of objectives, targets, and techniques will depend heavily on the accessibility of the various targets. A target that is vulnerable to a given form of informal penetration will be said to be "accessible" or "penetrable" to *that* technique. If a target were vulnerable to a number of forms of penetration at the same time, it might be described as being "highly accessible."

The penetration capability of the penetrator and the vulnerability or accessibility of the target are at times virtually the same thing. For analytical purposes, however, it is helpful to distinguish the two. When attention is directed toward the penetration capability of a nation, one side of the equation is examined. But when accessibility is being discussed, attention is focused on the other side—the target. It is also helpful to distinguish these two aspects of the relationship between penetrator and target when there are more than two nations involved. Nation A, for example, might be highly accessible to the penetration efforts of B and almost impervious to those of C. A, B, and C might be Indonesia, Communist China, and the United States, in that order. In such a case, the accessibility of A and the penetration capability of C would by no means be the same thing.

For some purposes, a distinction needs to be made between access and accessibility because not all targets that are accessible have, in fact, been penetrated. Nation B, for example, may have access to A, yet B may choose not to exploit its opportunity. For various reasons, B may wish neither to attack nor to support A. It may have only good will toward A, in which case it would not want to attack, and yet it may have no reason to offer A informal support. In this case, B would gain by neither attacking nor supporting A. The United States, for example, has a splendid basis for informal access to Canada, but has chosen not to exploit it.

The concept of accessibility is applicable to any target—a loose grouping, a formal organization, a decision-making circle, an industry, or a nation as a whole. For convenience, targets may be thought of as ranged along a scale of accessibility. If we are speaking of nations, at the lower end of the scale (being relatively inaccessible) are such countries as Japan prior to Admiral Perry's visit or the Soviet Union under Joseph Stalin. At the upper end are countries that are relatively open to penetration, such as France in the decade before World War II. The use of this scale indicates the accessibility of a target in overall terms. Precise analysis, however, would require more refined instruments. For example, a country that is highly accessible in general might be quite impervious to certain kinds of penetration. Conversely, one that is relatively inaccessible might still be highly vulnerable to a particular kind of penetration.

The position of a state along this scale will vary over a span of time, depending on its counterpenetration measures, its internal cleavages, and so on. It is important to distinguish, therefore, between *technical accessibility* and *substantive accessibility*. Technical accessibility relates to the actual mechanics of penetration. Can a radio broadcast actually be received in a country? Is it logistically possible to supply a guerilla movement in the target country? Substantive accessibility, on the other hand, involves the emotional and ideological response of the target population to the efforts at penetration.

Ignoring all refinements of degree, the two variables provide four possible types of relationship:

Case 1 would provide optimum conditions for penetration. In Case 2, the situation is ripe, but technical access is ineffective. If technical access were *wholly* ineffective, it would matter not at all whether the situation were ripe or not. However, if technical penetration were only partly successful but the situation very ripe, a good deal might still be accomplished. Case 3 involves the juncture of highly effective technical access with an unripe situation, not a promising combination. An example is the present effort directed toward the United States by the Soviet Union. No matter how effective the

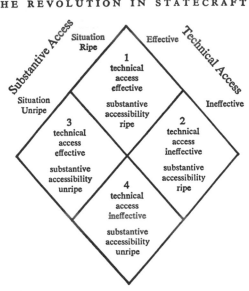

Figure 1.4

communication is technically, it falls on deaf ears. In Case 4, the situation is virtually hopeless from the viewpoint of the penetrator.

To do justice to the complexity of the situation, however, it is necessary to increase the number of variables dealt with. Technical penetrability, for example, has not one but two aspects. It involves not only the offensive measures of the penetrator but also the technical countermeasures taken by the target nation. Nation B may be broadcasting very well, but if Nation A jams those broadcasts, technical penetrability may be very low. By the same token, substantive penetrability also has two aspects. The target must be ripe if there is to be substantive penetration, but the message from the penetrating nation must also be adapted to the substantive vulnerabilities of the target. Fascist propaganda, for example, would not make much headway in England; pan-Arab propaganda would not get very far in Norway; and pro-Israel agitation would make few converts in Egypt. In addition, a nation might be ripe for one type of penetration but not another. A people who are susceptible to psychological warfare might be quite unready for agitation looking toward an armed uprising. Just as the government of the target country can take action to lower that country's technical penetrability, it can also take measures to reduce substantive penetrability. A program of social and economic reform, alteration of the land-tenure system, dismissal of unpopular officials, a propaganda program—all of these measures—would decrease substantive penetrability.

The objectives of a penetrating nation should be formulated with some regard for feasibility, which means, in practice, that attention must be paid to the type of access that already exists or that may reasonably be anticipated. Thus, if the penetrating nation lacks access to the armed services of the target nation, it should not aim at a military coup. If it lacks access to the labor movement, in all likelihood it will not have much success with a policy of fomenting strikes. And, if its access is limited on all fronts, then it must content itself with limited objectives.

The penetrating nation will normally have a hierarchy of objectives concerning a given target nation that range from the grandiose to the more modest. Typically it will work toward several of them simultaneously, and, if it becomes apparent that the maximum objective cannot be achieved, it will lower its sights. Depending upon the nature of its objectives, the penetrating nation will direct its attention toward certain targets in the nation to which it is seeking access: individuals, political parties, the military services, governmental agencies, the opinion media, segments of public opinion, strategic industries and services, unions, cultural groups, youth groups, veterans' organizations, and so on.

Next, there is the question of the *technique* to be used in achieving informal access to a target. Some techniques can be used for either attack or support. For example, the access provided by an economic aid program might be used to assist the host country in developing its resources. However, it might also be used to inject advisers into the governmental system in the hope of achieving dominance over the political and economic life of the country. Other techniques are almost always confined solely to attack functions—subversion, guerilla warfare, strikes—or solely to support functions.

The techniques of penetrating target organizations have been highly developed by the Communists. In a country they do not already control, the Communists seek to build up increments of power. They have learned that organizational conquest can provide such increments, and, therefore, they make a systematic effort to penetrate institutional targets. The power increment from the conquest of a particular group may be slight, but the cumulative influence acquired through a systematic campaign of organizational conquest may be great indeed. These institutions may involve the arts, the press, science, labor, business, the churches, youth groups, women's organizations, veterans' organizations, and so on. Therefore, when their resources allow it, the Communists will seek access to any organization or category of persons that might prove useful.

Communist objectives with regard to a given organization would depend on the situation. The maximum objective would be the domination of the organization so that it could be successfully manipulated. A more modest objective would be the neutralization of the organization in an effort to reduce the harm it might do to the Communist cause. A minimum objective would be to penetrate the organization in order to obtain reliable intelligence of its purposes and activities. On the other hand, if the leadership of the organization is so well entrenched that it cannot be replaced or undermined, the Communists may conclude that a competing organization ought to be established. Finally, if a field is unorganized, Communists will generally try to organize it.

The developing nations have become high priority

targets for informal penetration during recent years and provide a number of special problems for any nation seeking access to them. An emerging nation is characteristically undergoing major changes, on many fronts, in a telescoped period of time. The economy is changing; a variety of new technologies and skills are being introduced; the value system is being radically remade; family relations, relationships between groups, and status structure are changing; existing institutions are being altered or replaced; established ideologies are subjected to rapid erosion; social bonds are weakened; new political ideas quickly gain adherents, and new political leaders and organizations appear; established elites lose their confidence and their followings. Thus, throughout the whole of the society, ideas and established behavior patterns are in a state of flux. Confusion, disorientation, anxiety, and resentment are unavoidable in these circumstances. Exaggerated hopes are likely to alternate with exaggerated fears. The breakdown of accustomed norms creates a widespread feeling of frustration at the same time that it releases people from accustomed restraints. A tendency toward political extremism and violence and extreme actions is a natural response to this situation. Inevitably there will be a gap between the expectations of the populace concerning economic development and the actual rate of progress. The people's fervent desire for economic development, coupled with the frustration of disappointed hopes, can lead to explosive outbursts. It is difficult enough for an established, stable, democratic society to adjust to change in an orderly, peaceful way, but a society in transition—with the scars of the battle for independence still fresh, with no tradition of moderation and evolutionary change, with new and unstable political institutions—may tend to seek solutions based on violence and naked power. The group in power, having much to lose, may gravitate toward arrest, repression, and execution, while the groups seeking power may turn toward terrorism and the technique of the *coup d'état*. With the population and the leadership in an excited, anxious state, without a clear sense of where they are going yet eager for a decisive movement in some direction, the potential for access and manipulation is considerable.

Penetration efforts must be adapted to the target society if they are to be successful. A nation that would penetrate a stable society must adjust its efforts to the stability of that society. To penetrate a society in transition, the appeals that are made, the techniques that are used, the target groups selected, must all be appropriate to the conditions within that society. Those who are planning penetration must be aware of both the characteristics shared by the developing countries generally and the special characteristics of a given target.

The shared characteristics would include a rigid social structure and an undeveloped economic system. Labor will be unorganized or, if organized, controlled by the government. Political parties will be weak, narrowly based, personal instruments. Governments are likely to be unstable, unresponsive, personalistic, relatively inefficient, and perhaps corrupt as well. The military will either dominate the society or intervene periodically in public affairs, hampering the normal development of political institutions. All of these characteristics reveal opportunities for exploitation by an astute foreign power that is so inclined.

A systematic effort at penetration will usually center on certain elements in the population—typically the intelligentsia, the military, labor, the peasantry, goverment personnel, the political opposition—and hope to use these elements as levers to accomplish broader aims. The role of intellectuals in the society is usually important, since they provide much of its drive, energy, administrative skill, and technical and political leadership. They are relatively few in number, have a high rate of interchange among themselves, and tend to read the same journals and periodicals. As a group, the intellectuals are unusually accessible to ideas and appeals and are relatively easy to communicate with, both physically and semantically. They are generally located in the larger cities when they are not studying or teaching at universities, either at home or abroad. Since they are also strategically located in the society, their accessibility is important. If most of the intelligentsia are in sympathy with the government and feel committed to it, they are an important bulwark. Discontented, for whatever reason, they can do great damage.

Among the intellectuals, students are a particularly volatile and important element. In the emerging areas, the educated elite is small, and the university student of today may be a significant government official, journalist, politician, or military officer tomorrow. Consequently, access to these young people is crucial. Furthermore, as students, they wield powerful influence in their own right. They may organize a riot or a strike, storm a palace, or stone an embassy, and, for the government in power, they are often harbingers of worse to come. Thus the intelligentsia in general and the students in particular are usually important targets of Soviet or Chinese penetration efforts in a developing country.

As a target group, labor has certain advantages and disadvantages. For one thing, its numbers are rarely great in the emerging nations. And, if organized at all, it is not organized effectively. On the other hand, the vacuum created by the absence of organizations needs to be filled, and the Marxist-Leninist emphasis on class struggle and union activities has enabled the Communists to exploit this element of the population with some success.

The rural peasantry is usually poor, inarticulate, discontented, and desirous of more land. When it can be aroused, it is likely to be a powerful factor, but the penetrator will encounter difficulties in achieving access to it. For example, the Alliance for Progress is seeking to alert and energize the peasantry but is finding it difficult to make inroads.

The military plays a central role in the politics of most emerging countries and, on the whole, is a partisan of modernization.[2] It introduces new technologies, specialized training, improved means of transportation, effective communications, centralized administration, and some conception of the outer world. Nevertheless, it may, of course, be a politically conservative instrument, supporting a reactionary political regime or, perhaps, maintaining itself in power. Conversely, it can be a reforming element: it is sometimes a good channel for upward social mobility, for when the economy in a country is stagnant, the military life will likely attract a high proportion of the vigorous, the ambitious, and the gifted.

> These young men often come from the families of petty traders, small craftsmen, and cultivators of small holdings. Like their fathers, they are aware of the distance separating them from the rich and the political elite. Thus there is brought into a potentially powerful position in society a body of intelligent, ambitious young men, equipped with a modicum of modern technical education but with little sense of identity with politicians and businessmen.[3]

This chapter has introduced the concept of informal access, has subjected it to preliminary analysis, and has demonstrated some of the uses to which it may be put. It has concluded with a brief discussion of penetration in the new and developing countries. To gain historical perspective, however, it will be useful to examine the actions of some of the great powers as they bear on informal penetration.

Notes

[1] John Herz, *International Politics in the Atomic Age* (New York: Columbia University Press, 1959), p. 40.

[2] John J. Johnson, *The Role of the Military in Underdeveloped Countries* (Princeton, N. J.: Princeton University Press, 1962).

[3] *Ibid.*, p. 6.

CHAPTER II

Informal Attack:

The Nazi and Soviet

Experience

The informal attack activities of any nation do not just "happen." Underlying them is a body of doctrine. The soundness and the imagination with which that doctrine is formulated will have a direct bearing upon the operational success of the activities stemming from it. Nazi Germany and the Soviet Union were pioneers in the development of both the theory and practice of informal attack. Therefore, an examination of their activities in this field is a logical, and perhaps necessary, step toward an understanding of the role that informal attack plays in world politics.

A. THE NAZI EXPERIENCE

The conceptions underlying the Nazi use of informal attack had been worked out by Hitler over a period of years, and on occasion he spoke candidly of the influences that had worked on him. Important to him were "The Protocols of the Elders of Zion," and it did not trouble him that they were well-known forgeries.[1] In answer to a question, he once remarked that from the Protocols he had learned "political intrigue, the technique of conspiracy, revolutionary subversion, prevarication, deception, organization." [2] The psychological assumptions underlying the Protocols must have reinforced Hitler's own inclinations. Certainly, emphasis in the Protocols on violence, terrorism, secrecy, psychological warfare, and the use of foreign agents must have been grist for Hitler's mill. He also acknowledged that he studied revolutionary technique in the works of Lenin and Trotsky.[3] The parallels between the activities of the Communist International and those of Hitler's agents abroad are many.

Hitler assumed that conflict was perpetual and that there was an essential continuity among all forms of conflict. He did not distinguish sharply between war and peace:

> War is eternal. War is universal. There is no beginning and there is no peace. War is life. Any struggle is war. War is the origin of all things.[4]

He did not think of war primarily in terms of weapons and killing. "What is war but cunning, deception, delusion, attack and surprise?" [5] These are the characteristics of all conflict, of which war is only one form. If war consists of cunning, deception, delusion, and surprise, as well as weapons, then the possibility arises that cunning and surprise might *substitute,* to some extent, for weapons and armies. If armed force is sufficiently overwhelming, surprise and deception are not needed. Likewise, if surprise and deception are great enough, one might almost be able to dispense with force.

> There is a broadened strategy, a war with intellectual weapons. What is the object of war . . . ? To make the enemy capitulate. If he does, I have the prospect of wiping him out. Why should I demoralize him by military means if I can do so better and more cheaply in other ways? [6]

German military planning was freed by Hitler from a narrow concentration on weapons, tactics, logistics, and casualties. Indeed, Hitler rejected the idea of a sharp distinction between psychological factors and the strictly military factors. The doctrines of blitzkreig, for example, were based on a set of psychological assumptions quite as much as upon a set of military assumptions. The daring thrust due west across France toward the Channel after the breakthrough at Sedan was justified only on the assumption that the French general staff would be stunned and incapable of improvising an adequate counter, that the morale of the French troops would decline sharply as a result of confusion and defeat, and that a mood favoring capitulation could be created without killing many French soldiers.

The same considerations that guided Hitler's thinking about war guided his thinking about all conflict. The key to strategy lay in determining the factors that would induce the enemy to capitulate. This approach involves a subtle but important change, since it makes the psychology of the enemy the primary target. It is his state of mind rather than his objective situation that one must focus on. Instead of asking, "How do we defeat the enemy?" one asks, "How do we induce a defeatist state of mind in the enemy?" As Hitler put it, "How to achieve the moral breakdown of the enemy before the war has started—that is the problem that interests me." [7] An integral part of his plans was the softening-up of the enemy.

> The place of artillery preparation for frontal attack by the infantry in trench warfare will in the future be taken by revolutionary propaganda, to break down the enemy psychologically before the armies begin to function at all. The enemy people must be demoralized and ready to capitulate, driven into moral passivity, before military action can be thought of.[8]

The *coup d'état* played an important part in Hitler's thinking about informal attack. "I need revolutions," he said. "I have made the doctrine of revolution the basis of my policy." [9] This approach assumes, of course, that he would have substantial numbers of agents available. Where were they to come from?

> When I wage war, . . . in the midst of peace, troops will suddenly appear, let us say, in Paris. They will wear French uniforms. They will march through the streets in broad daylight. No one will stop them. Everything has been thought out, prepared to the last detail. They will march to the headquarters of the General Staff. They will occupy the ministries, the Chamber of Deputies. Within a few minutes, France, Poland, Austria, Czechoslovakia, will be robbed of their leading men. An army without a general staff! All political leaders out of the way! The confusion will be beyond belief. But I shall long have had relations with the men who will form a new government—a government to suit me.
>
> We shall find such men, we shall find them in every country. We shall not need to bribe them. They will come of their own accord. . . . No Maginot Line will stop us. Our strategy, . . . is to destroy the enemy from within, to conquer him through himself.[10]

Interestingly enough, all of these statements were made before Hitler became chancellor.

Hitler was sometimes carried away with his own ideas, but the direction in which he planned to move was clear. He was free from any inhibitions about treachery, deceit, and the use of power. "My great political opportunity lies in the deliberate use of power at a time when there are still illusions abroad as to the forces that mold history."[11] The Hitlerian approach baffled a man like Neville Chamberlain who accepted at face value the induced demands of dissident minorities and sought to satisfy the "legitimate requests" that Germany might make. He was accustomed to honorable dealing among honorable men. At the time of the Czechoslovak crisis, it would not have occurred to him that while he was hoping to satisfy the demands of the Sudeten Germans, Conrad Henlein, the leader of the Sudeten Germans, was under orders from Hitler to present a series of demands to the Czechoslovak government that could not possibly be satisfied. While Chamberlain thought in terms of formal, government-to-government relations, Hitler was using the techniques of informal access in half a dozen ways.

Hitler's ideas on informal attack began to take shape long before he came to power; it is not surprising, therefore, that he began to prepare the ground for these activities even before he became chancellor on January 30, 1933. By that date, there were political movements in a number of countries that accepted the symbols, ideology, and techniques of the German movement: the Svenska National-socialistika Partiet in Sweden; the Danmarks National Socialistika Arbejder Parti in Denmark; the National-socialistiche Nederlandse Arbeiderspartij in the Netherlands; the Breton Fascists in France; the Thundercross movement in Latvia; the Magyar Nemzeti Szocialista Part in Hungary; the Iron Guard in Rumania; and, of course, the Nazi parties in Danzig and Austria. Some of the Nazi efforts at setting up foreign adjuncts of the Nazi party, however, were short-lived.

> In South-West Africa the mandatory South African authorities had already noticed that *Reichs* and *Volksdeutsche* were organizing on a national socialist basis, with the special aim of having that former German colony given back to Germany. In the summer of 1934 an end was made to this activity. On July 11 it was decided to ban the *Hitler-Jugend* and the next day a raid was carried out on the party offices of the *Auslands-Organisation*, where a great quantity of documents were confiscated. Their contents spoke for themselves. Four months later the NSDAP was declared illegal in South-West Africa.[12]

Successful penetration requires vulnerability on the part of the target nation as well as effort on the part of the penetrating nation. France before the Second World War provides an almost classic case of vulnerability. The French viewed international politics in a way that was deeply colored by their views on domestic politics. Thus, the Left was drawn toward a pro-Soviet policy, while the extreme Right was attracted toward Nazi Germany because of Hitler's anti-Communism and his emphasis on authority. To them, Germany appeared to be a bulwark against Bolshevism. These divisions provided fertile ground for the growth of Nazi penetration activities.

The head of the network of penetration activities was Otto Abetz, a man with extensive contacts among prominent French leaders. Abetz saw to it that the Franco-German Society in Berlin entertained distinguished French visitors. French writers were asked by German publishing houses for the translation rights of their books. Other leaders received flattering invitations to conduct lecture series in Germany. Newspaper editors who might be approachable were offered heavy advertising by firms such as Bayer and I. G. Farben.

> These corporations had branches in France. And it was through these French companies that the newspapers received their subsidies in the form of advertising contracts at very fancy prices. However, more often than not, this advertising matter was never published after the contract had been signed.[13]

Abetz arranged for French journalists to have exclusive interviews with Hitler. In these interviews, Hitler would point out that he was a veteran, that he knew at first hand the horrors of war, and that he wanted only peace and understanding between France and Germany. Those of a pacifist bent found these declarations comforting. Over and over Abetz would argue that the Germans knew war only too well and that no one need fear Germany again. French veteran groups were invited to Germany to attend celebrations in honor of German veterans. Other veterans joined the *Comité France-Allemagne* and, through it, came into contact with Nazis.

The press was thoroughly penetrated. According to one journalist, Pierre Lazareff, each of the five largest

Parisian newspapers made it a practice to accept payments from foreign governments. To help disseminate Nazi propaganda in France, the Germans arranged for the establishment of a special news agency bearing the name *Prime-Presse*. This agency concentrated on making news items and photographs available to the provincial press.

The *Maison Brune,* an informal adjunct of the German embassy, was opened on the Rue Roquepine early in 1936. Its staff sought, in diverse ways, to contact and influence Frenchmen by sponsoring illustrated lectures on Germany, excursions, sporting events, and parties. It also served to coordinate the activities of the large number of German associations in France and to organize espionage.

German professional groups, controlled from the *Maison Brune* and the German Embassy, existed until the war not only in Paris but also in Metz, Strasbourg, Lille, Roubaix, Tourcoing, Rouen, Marseilles, Bordeaux, Lyon, Nice, Toulouse, and Grenoble. They constituted a network extending throughout the country.[14]

In addition, there were extensive economic ties between Germany and France. In 1935, for example, Germany was buying 42 per cent of France's iron ore, and powerful interests in France would have opposed a disruption of this tie. It is interesting that Pierre Laval was for some time a legal representative of the *Comité des Forges,* the French iron cartel. What started out as a purely commercial exchange, and apparently remained so to the French, became to the Germans an avenue of political access to the other partner in the exchange.

In 1933, Goebbels and Ribbentrop established a "non-governmental" organization at Erfurt known as the World Center for the Struggle Against Jewry. This was one of the sources of the flood of anti-Semitic literature that circulated in France and found a ready audience in the membership of such groups as *Action Française* and the *Croix de Feu*. Groups of this kind, with

which France was well supplied, did not need to be pro-
Nazi. It was sufficient for Otto Abetz and his colleagues
that they were violently anti-democratic and prepared
to go to any lengths to overthrow democracy in France.
In a group such as Jacques Doriot's *Parti Populaire
Français,* however, neo-Nazis did play a direct and important role.

In evaluating the role of Nazi access in France before
the war, it is clear that Nazi activities helped divide the
Right. By neutralizing the Right, an element traditionally nationalistic and militant, they tended to paralyze
France as a whole. When the militants in a country
cease being militant about the country's enemies, then
the nation as a whole is likely to relax. Many patriotic
Frenchmen failed to see the menace of Germany or saw
it too late, and those who did perceive it were prevented
by great national fissures from mobilizing their countrymen against the threat. Much of the credit for this pa-
ralysis of will must be given to effective Nazi use of informal access. Heinz Pol has observed, "Quantitatively
and qualitatively the system he [Abetz] had built up in
France . . . was unexampled." [15]

The *Anschluss* with Austria provides a dramatic example of how the Nazis used the tactics of informal
attack. Shortly after becoming chancellor, Hitler appointed Theodor Habicht, an Austrian exile, as in-
spector of the Austrian Nazi party. The Austrian Nazis,
with weapons and dynamite furnished by Germany, instituted a reign of terror, during which they blew up
government buildings and power stations and murdered
supporters of the Dolfuss regime. Hitler then organized
an Austrian Legion, which camped on the Austrian
border in Bavaria, ready to move into the country.

On July 25, 1934, 154 members of the S.S. Standarte
89, dressed in Austrian army uniforms, broke into the
Federal Chancellery and assassinated the chancellor,
while other Nazis seized the radio station and broadcast
an announcement of the resignation of Dolfuss. How-

ever, the rebels were unable to follow up these early victories, and government forces under Schuschnigg soon regained control of the situation. Thirteen of the rebels were later hanged.

Nevertheless, Hitler kept up the attack, combining formal pressure on the Austrian government with the techniques of informal attack. The result was the Austro-German agreement of July, 1936, which contained secret provisions in which Chancellor Schuschnigg agreed to provide amnesty for Nazi political prisoners in Austria and to appoint Nazi-inclined individuals to important positions.[16]

Throughout 1937, on an almost daily basis, the Austrian Nazis continued their bombings. Then, on February 12, 1938, Schuschnigg was prevailed upon to sign an agreement with Hitler providing that the ban on the Nazi party would be lifted and that two pro-Nazis would be appointed to the cabinet, Seyss-Inquart as Minister of the Interior and Glaise-Horstenau as Minister of War. With the acceptance of these terms by President Miklas a few days later, Nazi penetration was institutionalized. There were massive Nazi demonstrations and pro-Nazi riots. With the police in Nazi hands, there was no legal recourse. The processes of orderly government began to disintegrate.

Finally, Goering telephoned orders to Vienna on the evening of March 11:

> Listen carefully. The following telegram should be sent here by Seyss-Inquart. Take the notes.
> "The provisional Austrian Government, which after the resignation of the Schuschnigg Government considers it its task to establish peace and order in Austria, sends to the German Government the urgent request to support it in the task and to help it prevent bloodshed. For this purpose it asks the German Government to send German troops as soon as possible." [17]

When an official of Country A can dictate the very language that shall be used by the government of Country B in calling for the entry of A's troops onto its soil, informal penetration has reached an extreme point. President Miklas, under heavy pressure, appointed Seyss-Inquart chancellor, and, on March 13, the Anschluss Law was proclaimed, making the formerly independent country of Austria a province of the German Reich.

The role of informal access in the Nazi take-over of the Sudetenland and of Czechoslovakia as a whole is impressive. The captured archives of the German Foreign Office permit a detailed study of this sequence of events. In 1933, in the Sudeten areas of Czechoslovakia, the Sudeten German party was formed under the leadership of Konrad Henlein. In the next few years, it gained the support of nearly all Sudeten Germans. This party received secret financial support from the German Foreign Office and also took its direction from that source. Subsidies and instructions were normally transmitted through the German minister in Prague. A telegram from Eisenlohr, the German minister, setting forth the substance of his discussions with the leaders of the Sudeten German party, makes clear how thorough was the German control of this party as the climax of events approached:

1) Course of German foreign policy as communicated by Legation is to be sole determining factor for policy and tactical procedure of Sudeten German Party. My instructions are to be strictly observed.

2) If consultation with Berlin offices is necessary or desirable before any of Henlein's important propaganda declarations, this would be proposed and arranged through Legation.

3) All communications from Sudeten Germans to German offices are to pass through hands of Legation.

4) Henlein will have weekly contact with me and, if requested, come to Prague at any time.

Hope henceforth to keep Sudeten Germany Party under close control, which is more than ever necessary for coming developments in foreign policy. Please in-form Ministries concerned and *Mittelstelle,* and request support for this unified steering of Sudeten German Party.

Eisenlohr[18]

The tempo of events began to pick up sharply in September, 1938. There were daily disturbances and demonstrations by the Sudeten Germans, and everywhere there was the slogan, *Ein Volk, ein Reich, ein Führer.* When the Czechoslovak prime minister and minister of the interior asked the Sudeten German party to desist from further demonstrations, the request was met with a demand that the police be instructed not to show themselves at Sudeten German party demonstrations.[19] Next, on September 13, the Czech government declared martial law in many Sudeten German areas. The Sudeten German Party Executive Committee responded to this with a six-hour ultimatum to the Czech government that demanded the virtual withdrawal of Czech authority from the Sudeten area.[20]

Every indication of willingness to negotiate on the part of the Czech government served to precipitate even more extreme demands. On September 14, Henlein declared that the Sudeten Germans wanted to return to the Reich and that no power on earth could deter them from this course. Then, on September 17, Henlein fled from Czechoslovakia into Germany, where he was given help in organizing a Sudeten Free Corps. By September 21, this Free Corps occupied some Czech frontier towns.

The next stage was reached at Munich, on September 30, when the British and French signed an agreement providing for the cession of the Sudeten territories. This did not end the difficulties, of course, but simply changed their nature. After the occupation of the Sudeten German areas, which were of immense strategic importance, a pro-Nazi government was forced on the remainder of the country. German access to this new government was excellent, and the demands the Germans presented to it—that it reduce the size of the Czech army, make special trade arrangements with Germany, accept German guidance over its foreign policy —virtually extinguished it as an independent government. At the same time, Hitler began to deal directly with Slovak politicians and to encourage their separatist ambitions. The German Foreign Office prepared a draft of the telegram that Monsignor Tiso shortly thereafter sent to Berlin, in an abridged form, asking Germany to take over the protection of the Slovak state. The Slovak declaration of independence also was prepared at the German Foreign Office. Thus, on March 14, 1939, "independent" Slovakia was created. Approximately the same process operated in the area of Ruthenia. Finally, on March 15, Dr. Hacha, the president of Czechoslovakia, was induced to sign the documents that formally ended the life of his country. The *Führer* graciously expressed his willingness to take the Czech people under the protection of the German Reich. Thus, a combination of informal access, armed threat, and diplomatic pressure was used to end the life of an independent country while preserving many of the legal niceties.

The economic warfare measures of the Nazis show a good deal of ingenuity, although this was not a realm in which Hitler himself appears to have contributed very much. The two principal kinds of economic warfare the Nazis engaged in were the manipulation of foreign trade and exchange rates and the use of cartel agreements. In addition, the Germans also made great use of private businesses to promote the flow of intelligence, propaganda, money, and personnel. In the British Empire and Latin America, the outlets of Schering A.G. "were the foci of German political intrigue. . . ." [21] In Bolivia, "three-fourths of the big firms . . . [were] German and German propaganda flooded the country." [22] In Chile, "the party's espionage organization, including military intelligence . . ." was under the direction of the general manager of the Bayer Company. [23] This type of informal access is interesting, although its overall effectiveness should not be exaggerated. In any case, it involves the political exploitation of commercial relations rather than economic warfare as such.

The German government made special arrangements for those countries with which it did not have multilateral payments agreements. It established an inland account system (termed *aski* for *Auslander-Sonderkonten für Inlandshazlungen*) for the manipulation of foreign trade and exchange rates. This system involved an intricate network of multiple foreign-exchange rates. Germany would authorize the import of a given quantity of goods on the condition that the foreign exporters accept payment in the form of a special credit in reichsmarks in German banks. These reichsmarks, however, could be used to pay only for specified kinds of German exports. Germany might, then, offer to import at prices above world prices and in this way attract the goods it wanted. By maintaining strict control over exports, however, Germany was able to pay for imports with items of its own choosing. A Latin American country, for example, might sell copper to Germany at a favorable price only to discover it had no alternative but to accept payment in harmonicas or toys.

In short, the objective of the *aski* system was to import goods on terms favorable to the importing country and to pay for them with products of marginal value. It had the secondary advantage for Germany of providing avenues of informal access—in the form of military and trade missions—to the countries involved. The system was not aimed at damaging the economies of the exporting countries, although it may sometimes have had this result.

The German economic thrust into the Balkans was organized somewhat differently. Germany had multilateral foreign-exchange clearing agreements with the Balkan nations. Under these arrangements, a German importer, instead of purchasing the currency of the exporting

ing country in order to make payment, would make payments into the German central banks to the account of the exporting country. The funds in the central bank would then be used to pay German exporters. If trade were perfectly balanced between the two countries, there would be no need to purchase foreign exchange.

At the outset, this device was used to help encourage trade during the Depression. But Germany found another use for it. German importers, offering attractive prices, drew more and more Balkan exports to Germany, principally agricultural products. Since Germany was exporting very little, however, Balkan importers were not making payments into their central banks and, hence, Balkan exporters could not be paid. In a short time, therefore, Germany became a debtor nation, importing a good deal and exporting very little.[24] Thus, as in Latin America, the Balkan nations were forced to accept payment in goods for which they had little need, or they received no payment at all.

However, Germany's objectives in the Balkans were not purely economic. These nations were seeking to rearm, and their creditor relationship with Germany forced them to accept obsolete German war material in payment. Germany derived several advantages from this relationship. First, a country that buys arms from another country is likely to be dependent on that other country for ammunition and replacement parts. And a dependent country is easily subjected to political pressure. Second, wherever Germany sold weapons, it sent military missions to train personnel in the use of those weapons. At the same time, the German business firms operating in the Balkans served as sources of propaganda and agitation, as German firms did elsewhere.[25] Finally, Balkan firms doing business with Germany were placed under pressure to discharge Jewish employees and to contribute to local Nazi movements.

Cartels developed as a natural outgrowth of businessmen's interest in minimizing competition by regulating prices and output and by dividing markets. Some German firms, on their own initiative, may have adapted their policies to suit the nation's overall objectives, but it was not until after Hitler's accession to power that German industry was systematically used as an arm of the government's international operations. As it mobilized for war, the German government looked upon industry, with its international ties, as one more means by which it could strengthen Germany and weaken its future adversaries. Participation in cartel arrangements was designed to achieve several objectives: weakening prospective enemies by inhibiting the development of essential industries; obtaining the benefit of foreign research; and preventing the shipment of strategically important goods from neutrals to enemies. Magnesium, tungsten carbide, synthetic rubber, and optical glass were among the products seriously affected by cartel manipulation.[26]

The use of the *aski* system and the exploitation of cartel agreements illustrate the way in which a government able to think in unorthodox terms can convert routine private dealings across national boundaries into instruments of national policy. In both instances, arrangements that were straightforward and businesslike when initially developed took on a sinister aspect when the Nazis laid hands on them and began to use them systematically as tools of economic warfare. In both cases, while the government called the signals, the transactions continued to be conducted by private concerns.

The economic warfare measures of the Nazis represent a different type of informal access from those dealt with thus far. Their purpose was to achieve influence over the economic processes of the target country and leverage over certain kinds of economic decisions, rather than access to a segment of the population.

B. THE SOVIET EXPERIENCE

The Soviet leadership began to use informal penetration shortly after the Bolsheviks seized power in 1917. The establishment of the Communist International in 1919 provided the institutional support for, and direction to, this program. For this reason, 1919 is a good date by which to mark the beginning of the era of informal penetration. Since the Soviet leadership pioneered in this field, it is important to understand the thinking that has undergirded its approach to informal penetration and the sources from which this thinking stemmed.

It is often said that Communists have an advantage over their opponents because they are guided by Marxist theory in regard to both means and ends. However, Marx and Engels concentrated on the defects of capitalism, and, beyond a few generalities, they did not deal with the post-revolutionary situation. From a practical point of view, then, although their writings may act as sources of general inspiration, they cannot serve as sources of genuine guidance. Nevertheless, they do very well as ex post facto sources of authoritative justification for decisions already taken. If the devil can quote Scripture, so can a good Communist quote Marx, Engels, or Lenin in support of virtually any position he might choose to take.

When the dictator wishes to be harsh, he can refer to the hostility of the capitalist and socialist camps. When he wishes to speak softly, he can refer to "the well-known Marxist-Leninist doctrine of peaceful coexistence." When he wishes to discipline foreign Communists who want to go farther than he does on some matter, he assures them that they are guilty of "left-wing deviation." When others are more moderate than he chooses to be, he accuses them of "opportunism" and "right-wing deviation."

When Khrushchev succeeded Stalin, he reversed a

number of Stalinist doctrines, but theory had little to do with it. Theory did not dictate that Stalin pursue the policies he did, nor that Khrushchev reverse them, nor that Mao Tse-tung be happy or unhappy with them. Khrushchev could quote Marxist-Leninist scripture as effectively as Stalin, and Mao as well as Khrushchev, and Tito as well as any of the others. Stalin is said to have remarked once that paper puts up with anything written on it. In the same way, Marxist-Leninist theory puts up with any interpretation made of it. One need not be a brilliant student or Marxist scholar to be a great "theorist"; all one needs is the physical power to enforce one's interpretation. Joseph Stalin, for example, was short on intellect but long on power.

Marxist-Leninist theory is, therefore, a tool used by the dominant political leader to meet his needs, and it can be made to say anything that he wishes it to say.[27] For this reason, it says one thing in the territory controlled by Tito, something else in the Soviet Union, and something quite different in the Chinese People's Republic. The notion that politics in the Communist countries has been replaced by scientific Marxist-Leninist theory is myth and no more. Politics proceeds as before: it simply makes a deliberate and conscious use of theory as a tool for convincing the faithful. Theory does not determine policy but, rather, legitimizes decisions once they have been made.

The one area in which Leninist writings are genuinely suggestive is on matters relating to the seizure and retention of power. General propositions do not decide specific cases, however, so that even here the writings do not provide real guidance. They do shape the "style" of Soviet behavior, nonetheless. Immersion in Leninist writings will incline a Communist to approach a set of problems with one cast of mind rather than another.

The mode of life of Lenin and Stalin and scores of early Bolsheviks left an indelible imprint on the Communist approach to international relations and contributed greatly to the heavy reliance on informal attack. These men lived their formative years, and in some cases most of their lives, in an environment that was hostile. They were perpetually at war with that environment. Their thoughts gravitated naturally to questions of strategy and tactics, offense and defense, military actions, the seizure of power, terrorism, and tsaricide. Their discussions centered on ways to penetrate the police and the army, on the role of workers' groups in a revolutionary situation, and on the techniques of propaganda and agitation. Their heroes were likely to be revolutionists or terrorists—Lenin's own brother was executed for complicity in an attempt on the life of the tsar. They thought illegally and they lived illegally, when they were not in exile or in prison. Their day-to-day life might consist of smuggling weapons, organizing secret meetings, operating clandestine newspapers, evading the police, training new organizers.

Whether a movement should operate legally or illegally in a given situation was to be decided solely upon tactical grounds. In Lenin's mind, there was no presumption whatever in favor of legal activity. The technique of operating simultaneously on both the legal and illegal levels was used by Lenin over a period of years. The time he spent in the harsh school of exile politics taught him a great deal about the strategy of organizational conquest. The 1905 experience, and the 1917 coup, taught him lasting lessons about the role of surprise, the calculated use of deception, the means of identifying and striking at the nerve centers of a society, and other techniques of clandestine political activity.

Lenin's insights on political power are enshrined in his writings and, transmitted in this way, have become part of the conventional wisdom of the well-informed Communist. But there is little Marxism and not much socialism in the writings referred to most frequently. In terms of their operational impact on Leninist ideas about power, the influences of Machiavelli, Babeuf,

Blanqui, and Tkachev rank with that of Marx and Engels.

The fact that traditional Marxist terminology is used in the description and analysis of a situation does not mean that the substance of the analysis, or the resulting policy, is peculiarly Marxist. An analysis that uses such terms as "struggling masses," "proletariat," "capitalists," "imperialists," "vanguard of the proletariat," "wars of national liberation," "the Socialist Fatherland," and so on, reveals the political orientation of the analyst, but it does not make his analysis Marxist in any real way. He uses this vocabulary because of habit, orientation, or a desire to conform, but the analysis itself does not require the use of these terms. Once the operational equivalents of these terms are grasped—i.e., for "Socialist Fatherland" read the U.S.S.R.; for "vanguard of the proletariat" read the Communist party; for "workers' organizations" read Communist-controlled organizations—the argument almost invariably emerges as a straightforward power analysis. Whenever there is a dominant, or official, ideology in a community, questions of moment will be discussed in terms of that ideology, and decisions will be justified on the basis of it, whatever the real reasons may be.

Therefore, it is not Marxism but the absorption of Lenin's thinking about power that has aided Soviet planners in organizing informal attack. Similarly, it is not the lack of a Marxist ideology that handicaps the officials of Western nations in the Cold War struggle; it is the fact that they have not studied the strategy and tactics of power acquisition so long and carefully as have their opponents. The conspiratorial dimension is new to them.

This conspiratorial dimension, however, was not novel to the Soviet leaders. Political leaders who have shaped their outlook over a period of years in the hard school of a revolutionary struggle for power are not likely to change that outlook radically when they take over the official machinery of the state. Indeed, the acquisition of power will seem to them to validate the tactics they have used. Thus the Bolshevik leaders applied to the international scene the same tactics that had proved successful during the years they struggled for power in Russia. Stalin, the dominant figure in Soviet foreign policy for a generation, was the underground man *par excellence.* It is not surprising that the habits of mind of Stalin, the clandestine operator, strongly colored the thoughts of Stalin, the master of Soviet foreign policy. The conspiratorial approach, foreign to Western thinking about foreign relations, was second nature to the array of lesser officials who have influenced Soviet foreign policy since 1917.

The views on the "organizational question" that Lenin set forth in *What Is to Be Done?* in 1903, and that governed Communist activity during the protracted drive for power in Russia, are still the views that guide Communist thinking in virtually every country to which the Communists are seeking access. This seminal work describes the potential strength and influence of small but disciplined bands of revolutionaries, setting forth the doctrine that should guide them on the issue of legal and illegal activity as well as the principle of "democratic centralism," or rule from the top down. It also prescribes the role of the revolutionary and the necessity for absolute internal discipline. The bands of Communists established the world over since the creation of the Comintern in 1919 are lineal descendants of the first Bolshevik faction set up by Lenin in conjunction with this manifesto.

Thus, Communist ideas on the uses and limitations of terrorism began to take shape more than half a century ago, for the tactics of infiltration and organizational conquest absorbed Lenin's attention almost from the beginning of his career. Their techniques of propaganda, agitation, and clandestine publication go back to the days of *Iskra* (*The Spark*), the early underground newspaper Lenin was associated with. Their approach to the seizure of power, so well demonstrated by the coup in Czechoslovakia in 1948, has been part of the Bolshevik conspiratorial outlook since 1903.

Another important contribution that Lenin made to Soviet theory and practice in foreign policy was his doctrine of conflict. Like Hitler, he assumed that conflict was perpetual and that it simply changed its form from time to time. Politics might be replaced by war, but the former was as much a form of conflict as the latter. And, as forms of conflict, he argued, the two have a great deal in common. They differ one from another primarily in terms of targets and techniques, but the basic principles of strategy and tactics, offense and defense are much the same. In politics as in war, Lenin believed, the successful practitioner is the man who can, from the vast array of possible conflict techniques, select those that are appropriate to a given situation and time.

The absorption of this point of view by Soviet officials would encourage flexibility in shifting from one tactic to another, in shifting back and forth between offensive and defensive tactics, and in perceiving different conflict techniques as interchangeable. It would militate against Soviet officials making a sharp distinction between war and peace. The coming of war would mean that the military forms of conflict were now to achieve greater prominence, but it would not mean that the non-military forms of conflict would be abandoned. In practice, this meant that, although the Soviet Union was heavily engaged militarily during World War II, it never ceased to conduct political warfare activities. The end of the war would not usher in a period of "peace," in the sense that there would be an absence of conflict; it would simply mean that the non-military forms of conflict would become relatively more important and that war would be replaced by cold warfare. Techniques of violence would continue to play a role, as in guerilla warfare, but on a much more restricted scale.

The ideas on informal attack that Lenin and others developed during the long years before 1917 were put to work soon after the Revolution. Orders were given that the more promising of the war prisoners held by the Russians in 1917 were to be given political indoctrination and training before being returned to their homelands. By this means, Bolshevism was introduced into Hungary and led ultimately to the short-lived Communist dictatorship of Bela Kun.

The Communist International, or Comintern, was established in March, 1919. A close observer at that time could have had little doubt about its purposes and the direction it would take. And, by the end of the Second Congress of the Comintern, the path was unmistakably clear. The Conditions of Admission to the Communist International, approved by that Congress, became famous as the "Twenty-one Demands." They are quite illuminating.[28] The first condition is that all propaganda must conform to the program and decisions of the Communist International. Point Two requires that all reformists and centrists, i.e., those who are not approved by Moscow, must be removed from power. Thus, in the first two demands, it is made clear that *all* Communist parties were to be brought under the control of the Comintern, which meant, as a practical matter, under the control of Russia. Point Three instructs Communists everywhere to set up illegal organizations as well as legal ones so that both kinds of activity can be carried on. The fourth of the "Twenty-one Demands" calls for "systematic and energetic propaganda in the army," and the fifth calls for revolutionary work in the rural areas. Point Nine increases the number of targets for penetration by including trade unions, workers' councils, factory committees, and cooperatives. Point Fifteen stipulates that all party programs are to be approved by the Comintern Congress or the Executive Committee of the Comintern, and Point Sixteen decrees that the decisions of both those bodies are binding on all parties belonging to the Communist International. In Point Fourteen, it is made clear that Communists outside the Soviet Union owe their primary allegiance to the Soviet Union rather than to their own country and that they should try to sabotage any military action directed against the Soviet Union.

Both Point Eight and the "Theses on the National and Colonial Question" adopted by the Second Congress showed that the leaders of the Soviet Union wanted to control liberation movements in all colonial areas. Only after World War II did most Americans become aware of the explosive potential in the colonial areas of the world. In Communist thinking, however, it has been recognized since the publication of *Imperialism, the Highest Stage of Capitalism* in 1916. The terms of reference might vary from year to year, but the Comintern had a continuing interest in the colonial issue.

From the beginning, the Comintern was used as a means of advancing Russian national interests. Comintern leadership used a variety of lofty symbols and spoke altruistically of the interests of the world proletariat, always interpreting these interests to coincide with those of the Soviet Union. The terminology used was revolutionary, but the substance was always nationalistic.

By 1920, most of the central conceptions of informal attack that were to be used by the Soviet Union over the next four decades were in an advanced stage of development. The struggle against external enemies was perceived as a prolonged one, to be fought on many fronts, with the actions coordinated through the Executive Committee of the Comintern. The key penetration techniques were already understood, and the primary target groups—army, navy, police, peasantry, labor, intellectuals, parliament—had already been identified. The central organizational concept, that the disciplined national Communist parties were to receive strategic and tactical guidance from a Comintern dominated by the leadership of the Soviet Union, was fully mature.

Each change in the line of the Comintern over the years presented new problems and new opportunities for informal access to target nations. The concept behind the Comintern was bold, but the leadership, in practice, often left much to be desired. Tactics that were appropriate at one time and place might be inappropriate at another, but the leadership was often too doctrinaire and inflexible to adapt them. Despite its sophisticated doctrine and the immense amount of effort expended, the Comintern scored no major victories in the long span of years from 1919 to 1943. The plans were grandiose, but time after time the final victory slipped away. China, for example, was a high-priority target for penetration, and the Soviet Union achieved splendid access to the Chinese government following the secret conference between Adolf Joffe and Sun Yat-sen in Shanghai in 1923. When Sun Yat-sen returned to Canton, he was accompanied by two Soviet advisers, Borodin and General Galen-Bluecher, the latter an experienced guerilla leader. Borodin served as Sun Yat-sen's chief political adviser, and General Galen became chief military adviser to General Chiang Kai-shek. In the end, however, the working pact between the Communists and the Kuomintang did not hold together, and Chiang Kai-shek bloodily crushed the Communists.

The Soviet intervention in Spain during that country's Civil War (1936-1939), which held promise for a time, also ended disastrously. After several months of hesitation, the Soviet Union sent to Spain pilots, instructors, aircraft, and equipment—and, more significantly, international brigades of foreign Communists. The volunteer soldiers and technicians who composed these brigades were recruited from many countries, but principally from the United States and the nations of Western and Eastern Europe. Here, then, the agents of one nation recruited volunteers from several nations to launch an attack on a third nation. This use of foreign volunteers minimized the risk of formal involvement by the Soviet Union and the possible loss of face in the event that the intervention was unsuccessful.

The Soviet Union also sent a number of administrative advisers and a large number of G.P.U. agents to Spain. These agents became associated with official Loyalist police work, and, in addition, conducted investigations on their own, made arrests, and held executions. The persecution of socialists and anarchists opposed to the Communists was ruthless. The use of police persecution was combined with an equally ruthless use of Soviet military aid. Non-Communist fighting groups were denied arms, and the threat of a complete cessation of arms aid was used repeatedly as a club to gain concessions. The Soviet objective was to take over the Loyalist army, the police, the administrative services, and all labor and peasant organizations. In this way, when victory over the Franco forces was achieved, the country would automatically be under Soviet rule.

The purges that had begun in the Soviet Union were soon extended to Spain, however, and the pattern of Communist liquidation of socialists and anarchists was complicated by Communist liquidation of Communists. Intrigue and the fight for survival absorbed energies that should have been directed toward the struggle with the Fascist forces. The Spanish intervention does not, therefore, add luster to the Soviet record of informal attack.

Despite the doctrinal emphasis on colonial revolt, the Comintern never achieved a significant practical influence in the colonial world. It did not, for example, make much headway in Java or in British India. Its efforts in Japan and Turkey were not successful, and it never played a real role in the struggle for Irish independence. But the absence of major Comintern victories during the years from 1919 to 1943 does not mean that these years were wasted from the Soviet point of view.

Without the experience gained during those years and the development of trained personnel, it is doubtful that Communist organizations would have scored the successes they did during and after World War II.

The Soviet Union sought to take advantage of the outbreak of war in Western Europe in 1939 by fishing in troubled waters. Its intent can be seen in the "Directive for Future Work" sent to Tito by the Executive Committee of the Comintern on May 9, 1941.[29] According to this document, the Yugoslav Communist party was to use its special position to seize power, and the Soviet Union would, in turn, use its control of the party to direct the affairs of Yugoslavia. Informal access was thus to provide the means for overturning the government and for controlling its successor.

With the Nazi attack on Russia on June 22, 1941, the objective of seizing power became a secondary concern, and the organization of maximum resistance to the Nazis was paramount. In France, Italy, Yugoslavia, Greece, Albania, and other countries, the Communists came to play an important role in the resistance. The orientation, training, organization, and discipline that had previously characterized Communist opposition to established governments were now employed in resisting the Nazi occupying authorities. The Communists were able to effect a speedy transition because little had changed except the target of resistance.

The political potential of resistance organizations was never lost sight of, and, as the ultimate defeat of Nazi Germany became increasingly likely, greater attention was paid to the political implications of resistance. Just as the Soviet Union had fought ruthlessly for control of the forces resisting Franco in Spain in order to control the government of Spain once Franco was defeated, so now it fought to achieve Communist domination of resistance movements wherever they might be— Yugoslavia, Albania, France, Italy, Greece, and so on.

In Yugoslavia, the partisan forces of Tito gained ascendency over the Chetnik forces of Mihailovitch, and, in Albania, the forces of Enver Hoxha crushed those of Abas Kupi. In both cases, the partisan leaders became the heads of the postwar governments. However, in Greece although the plan was the same, the Communist attempt at a military coup in 1944 was defeated by prompt military action by the British. This did not end the struggle for power in Greece, for the guerilla forces that had withdrawn to the mountains in the north and to the territory of Albania, Yugoslavia, and Bulgaria renewed their offensive in the summer and fall of 1946 and scored important gains. When attacked by units of the Greek army, these forces would fall back across the border into the neighboring countries. But economic and military aid to Greece from the United States under the Truman Doctrine and the closing of the Yugoslav border to the guerillas by Tito led to the final death of the guerilla movement. This attempt of the Communists to assume power in Greece by means of an informal guerilla offensive was carefully coordinated with a Soviet diplomatic offensive in the United Nations.

After the war, Communist tactics shifted again. In the early postwar years, Moscow instructed the Western European Communist parties to forsake the armed seizure of power and to participate in existing governments instead. As a result, the Communists participated in the French and Italian governments from the time of the liberation until May, 1947. And, when they did leave, it was not of their own accord. The principal objective of this form of access was to achieve influence over the foreign policies of France and Italy.

In 1947, the Communist Information Bureau, or Cominform, was established as a successor to the Comintern and as a tool for combatting the Marshall Plan. The Cominform was to provide the organizational means by which Communists in the countries "threatened" by the Marshall Plan could oppose it under the direction of the Soviet Union. In Italy the leader of the

Italian Communist party, Togliatti, spearheaded the opposition to the plan, while in France the Communist-dominated labor union, the C.G.T., shared the spotlight with the party. The French Communist press and parliamentary faction also opposed the plan. In 1947 and 1948, as a means of sabotaging the Marshall Plan and French economic recovery, the Communists in France sponsored strikes in the mines, in the nationalized industries, and in the public services.

A similar pattern appeared when the European Communists mobilized to oppose the North Atlantic Treaty. Once again the elaborate machinery of informal access was put to work. There were strikes, demonstrations, letter-writing campaigns, visits by delegations to public officials and foreign embassies, and powerful attacks levelled against American "warmongers," such as Dean Acheson and Omar Bradley.

In February, 1949, the French Communist leader, Maurice Thorez, went so far as to indicate that, in the event of war with the Soviet Union, French Communists would owe their primary loyalty to that country. He was asked, "What would you do if the Red Army occupied Paris?" He replied:

> If the common efforts of the freedom-loving French do not succeed in bringing our country back into the camp of democracy and peace, if later our country should be dragged against its will into a war against the Soviet Union and if the Soviet Army, defending the cause of freedom and socialism, should be brought to pursue the aggressors onto our soil, could the workers and people of France have any other attitude toward the Soviet Army than has been that of the peoples of Poland, Rumania and Yugoslavia? [30]

The Communist coup in Czechoslovakia demonstrates a number of traditional Communist tactics plus several new ones and shows the way in which the various techniques can be used to reinforce one another. The Czechoslovak government-in-exile of President

Benes negotiated a mutual-assistance pact with the Soviet Union in 1945, and, on the return of the government to Prague, it initiated policies recognizing Soviet pre-eminence in Eastern Europe. Although the Communists were in a distinct minority in the coalition government that was established, they sought and obtained the significant Ministries of Information and the Interior, the latter including control of the police. A pro-Soviet general also became head of the army.

Following the elections of May, 1946, a new cabinet was created with the Communist Clement Gottwald as prime minister. In this new administration, scores of positions with access to key points in the government fell to the Communists. Political leaders who opposed the regime were prosecuted for alleged war crimes. Vaclav Nosek, Minister of the Interior, concentrated on transforming the police into an adjunct of the Communist party through selective recruitment, purging, indoctrination, and intimidation. However, his authorization of the forced retirement or transferral of several non-Communist police commanders in the Prague area precipitated a demand from the majority of the cabinet on February 13, 1948, that he reverse his action. A cabinet meeting was scheduled for February 20 at which the issue was to be discussed. On February 19, Valerian Zorin arrived in Prague to make arrangements, he said, for grain deliveries, and, throughout the crisis, his presence symbolized the proximity of Soviet power. When February 20 arrived and Nosek had not complied with their demand, twelve cabinet ministers offered their resignations to the president, who delayed accepting them.

The Communists responded with a manifesto asserting that the opposition parties were plotting a seizure of power in order to prevent a free election. Next, Nosek announced that the leaders of the National Socialist party had tried to sell state secrets to the British, and a number of arrests followed. During the day, trucks brought hundreds of reliable Communists into the city.

The "Workers' Militia," armed from secret stores of weapons, began to gather in the suburbs of Prague, and the radio urged citizens to be ready to repel the forces of reaction and called for the organization of Action Committees. These committees (actually organized secretly some time before) sprang up in factories, clubs, offices, unions, villages, youth groups, women's groups, and peasant organizations. They sought to take over every organization or community of which they were a part, and they enjoyed remarkable success. By that evening, the Communist-controlled police had taken over most of the important public buildings as a means of paralyzing governmental action.

The following day, February 21, Communist-sponsored mass meetings were held, and a delegation purporting to represent the workers of Czechoslovakia presented President Benes with a carefully prepared list of demands, including the demand that he accept the resignations of the twelve ministers and replace them with representatives of mass organizations—that is, with Communists. Benes refused, but the end was in sight.

On February 23, the police began arresting leading anti-Communists as Nosek made further charges that those arrested had been planning a seizure of power. By now, thousands of persons had begun to flee the country to escape arrest. Meanwhile, throughout the nation, the Action Committees continued their work, for their opponents had not been trained to combat this form of informal attack. The nationalized paper mills announced that they would not supply paper to the opposition press, and the printers' union announced that it could print nothing against the interests of the workers.

By February 24, the battle was lost, though not yet over. Action Committees took over the opposition newspapers, and the streets were dominated by Communist demonstrations. The power to govern had passed from the hands of Benes and into the hands of the Central Action Committee. Finally, on the 25th, Benes accepted the new Gottwald government, and it was all over. No better example exists of how the agents of one nation can use informal access to achieve the almost bloodless overthrow of a foreign government.

In a penetration campaign directed toward a particular target country, the use of front groups is a standard technique. The names of these organizations suggest how various are the target populations to which the Communists seek access. In Israel at one time, a list of the more important front organizations would have included:[31]

> The Israeli Peace Movement
> The Israel Communist Youth Organization
> The Federation of Democratic Women
> The Democratic Teachers
> The Democratic Lawyers' Association
> The Israeli National Committee for Peace
> The Academic Peace Committee
> The Arabic–Language Poets
> The Progressive Youth Circle
> The Circle of Friends of Arabic Progressive Literature
> The Israel–USSR Friendship League
> The Israel–Romania Friendship League
> The Israel–Bulgaria Friendship League
> The Israel–Czechoslovakia Friendship League
> The League for Israel–USSR Friendship Ties
> The Israel–Polish Friendship League
> The Arab Pioneer Youth of Israel

The larger front groups will often have their own publications, as a means of reaching members and occasional outsiders.

In addition to the front groups set up in individual countries as part of the informal attack campaign in these countries, there are also Communist-front groups that seek an international clientele. In these cases, a single group is used to penetrate more than one target population. A 1955 study on world-wide Communist propaganda activities prepared by the United States Information Agency included the following among the principal front organizations:[32]

World Peace Council—publishes the monthly journal *Horizons* in twenty-five countries and in thirteen languages, including English, German, French, Russian, Spanish, Italian, Chinese, Japanese, Bulgarian, Romanian, Portuguese, Finnish, and Persian.

World Federation of Trade Unions—publishes the monthly journal *World Trade Union Movement* in English, French, German, Russian, Spanish, Portuguese, Swedish, Romanian, Chinese, Japanese, and Hindi.

International Union of Students—publishes the monthly journal *World Student News* in English, French, German, Italian, Spanish, Russian, Norwegian, and Arabic.

World Federation of Democratic Youth—publishes the monthly journal *World Youth* in English, Russian, Spanish, German, Danish, Chinese, Italian, Polish, Hungarian, and Romanian.

Woman's International Democratic Federation—publishes the monthly journal *Women of the Whole World* in English, French, Russian, Spanish, and German.

World Federation of Scientific Workers—publishes the semiannual journal *Science and Mankind* in English, French, Russian, and Chinese.

International Organization of Journalists—publishes monthly *The Democratic Journalist* in English, French, German, Russian, and Spanish.

International Broadcasting Organization—publishes a quarterly journal the *Information and Documentation Bulletin* in English, French, Russian, and Chinese.

International Federation of Resistance Fighters—publishes the journal *Resistance Unie* every two months in French and German.

Committee for the Promotion of International Trade—publishes the monthly journal *International Trade* in English and French.

World Congress of Doctors—publishes the quarterly *Living Conditions and Health* in several languages.

Some of these organizations, such as the International Union of Students and the World Federation of Trade Unions, have subsidiary organizations that also have their own publications.

For many years, the Soviet leadership has been aware of the importance of what has come to be called "cultural diplomacy." [33] During the 1930's, scores of organizations, similar in many respects to those already mentioned, were created as instruments of the cultural offensive. The objective was to establish contact with academic, artistic, scientific, and other groups in the target area, and, through these groups, to achieve a degree of access to their membership. The access could be used for many purposes, including the creation of a more favorable image abroad of the cultural and intellectual life of the Soviet Union.

Throughout the 1920's and the 1930's, the Soviet hierarchy devoted much attention to wooing distinguished foreigners who visited the U.S.S.R. Deception and selective presentation of fact were nicely combined with appeals to the idealism and hopes of the visitors. Even forced collectivization and the purges did not render this technique ineffective. The list of impressionable visitors is a long one and includes such persons as Sidney and Beatrice Webb, Lincoln Steffens, Maurice Hindus, John Dos Passos, André Malraux, and André Gide. Some of these visitors retained their enthusiasm for Communism for years, while others soon lost it.

Toward the end of the 1930's, the Soviets were involved in cultural exhibitions abroad, and, by the late 1950's, they could be counted on to participate in many international exhibitions. Large-scale educational exchange programs are a recent innovation, but they have rapidly become an important part of Soviet cultural activity. These exchanges have concentrated on students from African and Asian nations. (It may be misleading, however, to speak of these programs as "exchange" programs since the traffic tends to be one way. For both political and educational reasons, there are few Soviet students traveling to the Afro-Asian nations for their education.) On the whole, these programs appear to have been quite successful, although there have been a number of cases of friction. In the last few years, for example, there have been frequent reports of dissatisfaction (and even rioting) by African students in the Soviet Union who felt that they were being subjected to racial discrimination.

Despite the long-term increase in Soviet cultural activities abroad, the program has seen wide fluctuations from year to year. For example, just prior to the 1955 summit conference, cultural interchange reached a peak and then dropped rather sharply. But, since the emergence of the Sino-Soviet split, the level of cultural exchange has risen once more. There is no guarantee that it may not decline again, however. The reason for the fluctuation is that the Soviet leadership does not view cultural exchange as a good in itself. Therefore, the program cannot be thought of as autonomous, operating independently of the vicissitudes of Kremlin thinking on foreign policy. Nor are the Soviet leaders trying to maximize cultural exchange as a road to improved international understanding; instead, they are trying to maximize Soviet benefit from it, which is by no means the same thing. When the leadership calculates that Soviet interests will be advanced by it, there will be an increase in cultural activities. And they may be cut back just as abruptly. The cultural activities of other nations also have a national interest element behind them, but they are rarely manipulated in so abrupt, disciplined, and calculated a manner.

Despite its work in the field of cultural diplomacy, the Soviet Union, on the whole, has been less farsighted and imaginative in its use of informal support measures than in the development of informal attack techniques. For one thing, its record in the use of economic aid is not impressive. For years, its expenditures for such aid and for technical assistance were at a modest level; then they declined during the period from 1959 to 1963. In spite of the aid it had given, the Soviet Union had been rebuffed by the Congo and Guinea, and Communists in Iraq had been persecuted. This led to a reassessment of the utility of foreign aid.

In late 1963, there were indications of a reversal of policy, however, and aid figures rose sharply in 1964. It appears that the annual Soviet aid figure may reach $500 million. This reappraisal of foreign aid and the consequent loosening of the purse strings appear to be closely associated with the split between the Soviet Union and China. This rivalry has taken many forms including that of a struggle for influence and support among the neutralist nations. Soviet interest in Algeria, for example, showed a notable upturn after the Chinese government began to curry favor with the insurgents both before and after they became the legitimate government. Furthermore, the readiness of the Soviet Union to provide economic and military aid to India is, without doubt, a response to Chinese interest in that subcontinent. For example, the Soviets have undertaken the building of a sizable steel plant at Bokaro, and weapons, such as ground-to-air missiles and air-to-air missiles, have been sent to India. Not all Soviet economic aid can be explained in terms of the Sino-Soviet rivalry, of course. The building of the Aswan High Dam in the United Arab Republic and the aid given to Iran, Yemen, and Kenya, for example, can be explained in other terms.

Economic aid and technical assistance are apparently now viewed by the Soviet leadership as more important instruments of foreign policy than they once were. Their use of informal penetration no longer relies to so great an extent on the standard forms of attack, such as the use of Communist parties and front groups. Instead, they now supplement these measures with such support measures as economic aid, military aid, technical assistance, and cultural diplomacy. Part of the explanation for the change lies in the fact that the Soviet Union has more friends than it once had. A powerful nation will seek to support its friends and attack its enemies. On the other hand, a nation that is virtually friendless (and ambitious) has no alternative but to specialize in attack. Certainly the change makes informal penetration a more versatile and effective weapon in the hands of the Soviet leadership.

Throughout the early 1920's, the threat of the Soviet Union to non-Communist nations was primarily ideological. It had developed sophisticated doctrines of informal attack, but it lacked the organizational resources, at home and abroad, to put these doctrines to work. The appeal of Marxist ideology remained powerful during the early and middle 1930's, but the organizational resources devoted to informal attack were substantially increased. By the late 1930's, the increasing strength of the Soviet Union, as a nation, began to play a more important role in its search for power and influence. Since World War II, the sheer power of the U.S.S.R., rather than the ideological appeal of Communism, has been the major factor in most Soviet successes.

With the passage of years, it became so obvious that the requirements of Soviet foreign policy dominated the revolutionary ideology that the latter lost much of the effectiveness of its appeal in Western Europe, the United States, and parts of Asia. The decline of the ideological appeal of Communism reduced, at the same time, the effectiveness of the informal attack techniques that rely on ideology—radio, party press, and so on. The growth of the Soviet power base undoubtedly represented a net gain in the capacity of the Soviet Union to threaten other nations, but this gain was purchased at the cost, so to speak, of a decline in the ideological appeal of Communism and in the effectiveness of its informal attack techniques. If the three factors—ideological appeal, informal attack, the Soviet power base—had consistently supplemented each other, the Communist threat would have been far greater than it was.

In comparing the informal attack activities of Nazi Germany with those of the Soviet Union, it must be borne in mind that the life span of the first regime was only a fraction of that of the second. Hitler came to power in January, 1933; war began in September, 1939; he took his life in April, 1945. The entire cycle of the Third Reich was thus completed in twelve years. The Soviet regime, in contrast, has been in power for close to five decades. It has had half a century in which to refine its informal attack doctrines and improve its operating techniques.

Like Lenin, Hitler believed in the continuity of different forms of conflict. Unlike Lenin, however, he was oriented almost exclusively toward war. His thinking was geared to war and his informal attack activities were, in their more important aspects, adjuncts to his plans for eventual war. He was more successful in conducting a war of nerves than was Stalin or Khrushchev, and the Nazis also had greater success with economic warfare techniques than the Communists have had. In the use of dissident national minorities, both regimes were skilled, although they operated in somewhat different ways, and each had a different basis for its lateral appeal to persons inside the territory of other states. Both were successful in establishing disciplined groups abroad to serve as instruments for their purposes. The Nazis made skillful use of front groups, but the Communists have demonstrated that they are the true masters of that art. Again, the Communists have been more successful in the colonial areas, a field in which Hitler had little interest.

Both movements scored successes by means of informal attack, but the Communists were undoubtedly more successful in combining ideas and techniques providing long-term effectiveness. Just as Hitler was oriented toward war in his foreign policy, so he placed great emphasis on violence and intimidation in his informal attack activities. The Communists, using techniques that depend more on conviction than coercion, have had a much more stable base from which to operate. Even if war had not intervened, it is improbable that the Nazi overseas adjuncts could have maintained their effectiveness over an indefinite period. Hitler's informal attack apparatus, like his military machine, was not designed for a sustained, long-term effort.

It is interesting to note that both of the regimes that pioneered in the development of informal attack techniques came to power and consolidated their positions by the use of irregular means. They found it natural and easy to apply in other countries techniques similar to those they had used in capturing the instruments of state power in their own countries. Part of the explanation, then, for the speed with which they developed the doctrine and practice of informal attack against other countries lay in the years of experience that each movement had had before coming to power.

Notes

[1] Herman Rauschning, *The Voice of Destruction* (London: G. P. Putnam, 1940), pp. 238-241.

[2] *Ibid.*, p. 241.

[3] *Ibid.*

[4] *Ibid.*, pp. 6, 7.

[5] *Ibid.*, p. 97.

[6] *Ibid.*, p. 7.

[7] *Ibid.*, pp. 9, 10.

[8] *Ibid.*

[9] *Ibid.*, p. 11.

[10] *Ibid.*, pp. 7, 8.

[11] *Ibid.*, p. 103.

[12] Louis de Jong, *The German Fifth Column in the Second World War* (London: Routledge and Kegan Paul, 1956), p. 9.

[13] Pierre Lazareff, *Deadline* (New York: Random House, 1943), pp. 108-109.

[14] Heinz Pol, *Suicide of a Democracy* (New York: Reynal and Hitchcock, 1940), pp. 116-117.

[15] *Ibid.*, p. 97.

[16] *Documents on German Foreign Policy, 1918-1945* (Washington: Government Printing Office, 1957), Series D, I, pp. 278-281.

[17] William L. Shirer, *The Rise and Fall of the Third Reich* (New York: Simon and Schuster, 1960), p. 342.

[18] *Documents on German Foreign Policy, 1918-1945* (Washington: Government Printing Office, 1957), Series D, II, pp. 169-170.

[19] *Ibid.*, p. 745.

[20] *Ibid.*, p. 751.

[21] Joseph Borkin and Charles A. Welsh, *Germany's Master Plan* (New York: Duell, Sloan, and Pearce, 1943), p. 144.

[22] Graham Stuart, "Totalitarian Activities in South America," *Institute of World Affairs Proceedings*, XIX (1941), p. 62.

[23] Hugo Fernandez Artucio, "Chile, Norway of South America," *Free World*, II (March, 1942), p. 172.

[24] See Paul Einzig, *Bloodless Invasion* (London: Duckworth, 1939), 2nd. ed., for a discussion of Germany's economic warfare tactics.

[25] *Ibid.*, pp. 64-65.

[26] See Ervin Hexner, *International Cartels* (Chapel Hill: University of North Carolina Press, 1946). Also Joseph Borkin and Charles A. Welsh, *Germany's Master Plan* (New York: Duell, Sloan, and Pearce, 1943).

[27] Andrew M. Scott, *The Anatomy of Communism* (New York: The Philosophical Library, 1951), chapters V, VI, VII.

[28] *The Communist International, 1919-1943, Documents*, Jane Degras, editor (London: Oxford University Press, 1956), I, 166-172.

[29] Stephen Clissold, *Whirlwind: An Account of Marshal Tito's Rise to Power* (London: Oxford University Press, 1956), pp. 166-172.

[30] *The New York Times*, February 23, 1949.

[31] *Target: The World, Communist Propaganda Activities in 1955*, Evron M. Kirkpatrick, editor (New York: Macmillan, 1956), p. 228.

[32] *Ibid.*, pp. 33-34.

[33] See Frederick C. Barghoorn, *The Soviet Cultural Offensive: The Role of Cultural Diplomacy in Soviet Foreign Policy* (Princeton, New Jersey: Princeton University Press, 1960). See especially chapters IV-IX.

CHAPTER III

The Revolution
in American Statecraft

The history of any great nation is ambiguous. Thus the history of the United States is sprinkled with examples of a crude use of power in foreign policy—against the Indian tribes, against Mexico and Spain in the interest of territorial expansion on the North American continent, against the Latin American nations. The era of the Big Stick is not long in its grave. The United States occupied the Dominican Republic from 1916 to 1924, Haiti from 1915 to 1934, and Nicaragua almost continuously from 1912 to 1933.

Yet, in seeming contradiction, historians are fond of pointing to a lofty moral element and to a tradition of self-abnegation in American foreign policy. Non-entanglement as an ideal traces back to George Washington's Farewell Address. Woodrow Wilson's strictures on power politics struck a responsive chord among the American people as did the set of attitudes underlying the Fourteen Points. Franklin Roosevelt's enunciation of the Good Neighbor policy was popular in the United States, and the doctrine of non-intervention seemed eminently just to most Americans. As the end of World War II drew near, a great many Americans assumed that the postwar years would usher in an era of good feeling. The establishment of the United Nations at San Francisco enforced this expectation of a world without power politics. As appropriate to such a world, the United States quickly dismantled the bulk of its military manpower when the fighting ceased.

Both of these strands in the American foreign policy tradition—the use of power and the abhorrence of power—can be traced through the postwar years. Their interplay had a strong influence on the way the United States responded to the situation in which it found itself. The American view of power, and the way that it related to war and peace, made it difficult for the United States to grasp some of the power realities of the mid-twentieth century. Whereas Nazi doctrine and Marxist-Leninist doctrine treat war and peace as simply different parts of a conflict continuum, the American approach treated war and peace as mutually exclusive. "War" called for a maximum, unrelenting effort, with no holds barred. "Peace" meant the absence of violence, the absence of conflict and struggle, the absence of a deep involvement in foreign affairs, and a happy absorption in peacetime activities. The rumblings of the war had scarcely died away, however, before the more alert American observers began to realize that the postwar world did not quite fit their expectations. Instead of living in a power-free world of nations associated in harmony and equality under the aegis of the United Nations, the United States found itself drawn into an undesired, unprecedented, and little-understood conflict with a strong, ingenious foe who was playing for the highest of stakes.

American leaders faced opponents who assumed instability and conflict, not stability and harmony; who thought in terms of the illegal acquisition of power rather than the legal; who relied on coups, assassination, guerilla movements, front groups, deception, and infiltration rather than on the vagaries of elective politics. It is as if, perhaps, a visiting baseball team arrived at a ballpark to discover that their opponents had shot the umpire, poisoned the water, mined the basepaths, and were preparing to drop grenades into the dugout. While Harry Truman was training in courthouse politics in Missouri, Joseph Stalin was training as a professional revolutionary, living a life of clandestine meetings, pseudonyms, terrorism, arrest, and exile. While Dwight Eisenhower was learning about life from the vantage point of peacetime military bases in the United States, Nikita Khrushchev was learning how to survive and rise to the top in a more competitive environment—the Communist party of the Soviet Union. While John Fitzgerald Kennedy was learning the ropes in the Congress of the United States, Gamal Abdel Nasser was seizing power in Egypt, Ho Chi Minh was running the French out of Indo-China, and Fidel Castro was leading a group of bearded rebels in the Sierra Maestre Mountains of Cuba. While Lyndon Johnson was a boy in Texas, Mao Tse-tung was leading the Long March and developing the ideas on guerilla warfare that were to bring the Communists to power in China (and elsewhere) and were to overturn the equations of power throughout the world. It is significant that so many of the leaders who placed a heavy reliance on informal attack were trained in revolutionary tactics or came to power by leading a revolutionary movement or participating in it. It could not fail to be interesting, also, to see how leaders trained in a stable society with regularized political processes would cope with opponents possessing such a markedly different outlook.

As American opinion, both public and official, became aware of the Soviet challenge, attention began to center on the response that the United States should make. Soviet tactics and ambitions had to be resisted, but how was this to be done short of war? The first articulate statement of the problem and of the general lines of the American response came in July, 1947, with the publication of George Kennan's article, "The Sources of Soviet Conduct." [1] In this piece, Kennan counseled a "long-term, patient, but firm and vigilant containment." The decision to contain the Soviet Union represented progress, but it left to be discovered the policies and programs that would accomplish this goal. Policies normally associated with war were unacceptable while those normally associated with peace were irrelevant. Traditional statecraft was at a loss to deal with a situation that was neither war nor peace, and, for a short time, American policy-making was at an impasse. A new set of policies, programs, techniques, and instruments had to be developed if the challenge was to be met.

The story of the American response to the Soviet challenge and to a number of the other problems of the postwar world is largely the story of the development and use by the United States of an array of techniques for informal attack and informal support. This chapter will deal briefly with some of the highlights of that story.

While the United States had never before faced a peacetime challenge of this nature or magnitude, there were nevertheless certain kinds of experience it could draw upon. For one thing, it was able, in a limited way, to draw upon its own previous interventionist experience, particularly in Latin America. And it was able to learn a good deal by studying the operations of the Soviet Union. But perhaps the most useful body of experience was that gained by American civilian and military officials during the war. Once Americans realized that war and peace were not mutually exclusive in an era of Cold War, they were able to examine wartime activities and learn from them. Army occupation officers were not engaged in informal penetration since their occupation authority was formal and official, yet some of them did learn to analyze the problems of other societies and to shape developments within them. In addition, American officials had a number of politico-military experiences during the war that were capable of providing lessons if they were examined with this in mind.

The American experience with the United Nations Relief and Rehabilitation Administration also proved valuable. UNRRA was oriented toward relief—the provision of food, clothing, and fuel—rather than reconstruction, but if American administrators had not had to grapple with relief problems for several years, they might not have been able to achieve the broader and longer perspectives later embodied in the Marshall Plan and in Point IV.

Most of the informal access techniques developed by the United States since the war have been associated with the Cold War. However, some antedated this conflict, and others were only indirectly concerned with it. In 1946, for example, before the Cold War had taken a form that was widely recognized, Congress voted a $3.75 billion loan to Great Britain. Tied to the loan were stipulations concerning the currency convertibility policy that Britain was to follow. By virtue of the loan, therefore, the United States achieved influence over a portion of Britain's financial policy. There were other substantial American loans to European nations at the same time, but no attempt was made to use the leverage generated by them to insist on coordination of economic policy among the recipient nations or on particular economic policies within those nations. However, although these loans were not effectively used to create informal access, the lesson was soon to be learned.

The acknowledgment by Great Britain that it was financially incapable of continuing its role in Greece and Turkey created a crisis for the American government. Before a joint session of Congress on March 12, 1947, President Truman outlined the situation and the actions he proposed to take. He asked for $400 million to send economic and military aid to Greece and Turkey and to finance civilian and military personnel who could help in the reconstruction of the two countries. With this program for Greece and Turkey, the pattern of informal support that the United States was to use over and over again in succeeding years can be seen in a recognizable form for the first time—the transfer of American resources tied in with advice and assistance of many kinds.

The economic crisis was not confined to England but plagued countries on the Continent as well. A cluster of severe problems—inflation, low production, and balance of payments difficulties—was producing a progressive economic collapse in Western Europe. Among the political consequences of the breakdown was the rapid growth of continental Communist parties. Once again the United States chose to act because the consequences of inaction would be intolerable. The Marshall Plan was evolved, and, in due course, a massive transfer of resources to Europe began.

The transfer of economic resources did not, in itself, provide informal access. But access was achieved when the aid was associated with advice and guidance. Before long, thousands of American administrators, economists, technicians, and businessmen were concerning themselves with the economic and political life of Western Europe. If some of these advisors were preoccupied with peripheral questions, others were concentrating on economic and political issues of central importance. During this relatively brief span of years in which the United States was transferring billions of dollars of resources annually to Europe, informal American influence in the counsels of the European nations was enormous. For various reasons, the extent of this influence may never be fully chronicled.

From the beginning, United States aid was made conditional upon a high level of cooperation among the European nations. The Committee for European Economic Cooperation (CEEC) of 1947 became the Organization for European Economic Cooperation (OEEC) in 1948 and was given the task of recommending how the aid funds of the United States were to be allocated. But, of course, the final decision on allocation remained with the United States. The exchange of information within the OEEC on the part of the participating nations was unprecedented. They shared information on the functioning of their economies and their industries that had long been secret. In addition to the more or less continuous exchange of economic data, there was an annual review during which the programs, problems, prospects, and projected aid requests of each country were scrutinized by each of the other countries. As the OEEC nations tried to develop agreed recommendations on the allocation of U.S. aid, the officials of each nation achieved a degree of informal access to the economic decision-making machinery of the other nations. American officials, of course, received full information about the economies of all the recipient countries and played an active role in all discussions. Through the medium of the OEEC, as well as bilaterally, the United States participated in the economic decision-making of virtually every country in Western Europe.

This participation was not merely that of a friendly but neutral observer. The objectives of the United States, as they evolved over time, were extremely ambitious and looked toward nothing less than the economic remaking of the Continent. Leading American officials were intent on breaking down national barriers to trade and creating one vast European market. As a means to this end, they sought a vast expansion of intra-European trade, the achievement of currency convertibility, and the reduction or elimination of exchange controls, import quotas, and tariffs. In addition to pressing for the modification of governmental controls, American officials also sought to modify the structure of industry itself, ending cartelization and introducing the religion of mass production. American businessmen also advised their European counterparts on matters of production, marketing, and labor-management relations.

The insistence of the United States on a regional approach to European problems gave a great impetus to regionalism. Its pressure was exerted formally and informally, and it included persuasion, coercion, and inducement. The European Payments Union provides a case in point. The EPU promoted intra-European trade by allowing individual nations to balance their trade with the entire group of European nations rather than forcing them to balance bilaterally at a lower level of trade. The EPU, which played an important role in the European recovery, owed a great deal to American initiative and was established with funds provided by the United States.

In May, 1950, French Foreign Minister Robert Schuman proposed the formation of a European Coal and Steel Community. American interest in European economic cooperation had paved the way for the proposal, and, later, American counsel and informal support played an important role at almost every stage in the development of the Coal-Steel Community. In May, 1952, the same six nations that belonged to the Coal-Steel Community—France, the Federal Republic of Germany, Italy, Belgium, the Netherlands, and Luxembourg—signed a treaty for the establishment of a European Defense Community. The conception was extraordinarily bold, both in its general ideas and detailed workings, but it was ultimately rejected by the French Assembly in August, 1954. However, the role of American informal influence was great in the events leading to the enunciation of the idea, in drafting the treaty, and in pressing for its ratification.

For the achievement of more modest objectives, "counterpart" proved a helpful instrument of informal access. According to this concept, a nation receiving aid was required to establish a local currency fund equal in amount to the dollar aid it received. This local-currency "counterpart" of the aid was generated by the recipient government's sale of the aid materials to their nationals. Up to 5 per cent of these funds were to be used for the administrative expenses of the European Cooperation Administration (ECA) and for the purchase of strategic materials. The remainder, which could be released only with ECA approval, was to be used where it would have the greatest effect on recovery and stability. The decision on the use of the funds—for housing, debt retirement, or whatever—would be taken after consultation with officials of the recipient nation and after an examination of that nation's economic, financial, and political situation. Counterpart thus provided officials of the United States with vast sums of the currency of other nations that they could spend in those nations as they chose—an instrument of informal access of no small importance.

The United States was a towering force on the European Continent in the late 1940's and early 1950's, and its ability to exert an informal influence on events and decisions was immense. It is important to note, however, that while the actions taken by the United States were in accord with what it conceived to be its own long-range historical interests, it defined these interests in such farsighted terms that they coincided to a great extent with the interests of the European nations. History provides few examples in which a powerful nation has acted toward weaker nations with greater wisdom, generosity, and forbearance. At a time when the United States dominated the Continent politically, economically, and militarily, it sought to lay the foundations for the birth of a new and stronger Europe. It assisted mightily in the economic recovery of Europe and, at the same time, played an important role in the modification of the structure and functioning of the national economies. Without America's formal and informal pressures for European integration, the European Economic Community might never have become a reality and the progress that has been made toward political integration might never have taken place. Economic recovery and the changes associated with it also had other important political consequences, such as restoring a degree of political stability on the Continent and replacing the traditional enmity of France and Germany with cooperation.

The problems of the emerging areas first received serious attention from the United States when President Truman, in his 1949 inaugural address, announced "a bold new program for making the benefits of our scientific advances and industrial progress available for the improvement and growth of underdeveloped areas." The Point IV Program, as it came to be called, was bold, but it was not altogether new. Technical assistance had been used in the European Recovery Program. Furthermore, the Institute for Inter-American Affairs, headed by Nelson Rockefeller, had been engaged in technical assistance in Latin America since early in World War II. The IIAA, which concerned itself primarily with agriculture, education, and public health programs, would operate in a country through a service agency to which both the local government and the United States contributed personnel and financial resources. With the Point IV Program, however, technical assistance was widely recognized for the first time as an important instrument for helping the developing nations. It is helpful, of course, precisely because it provides the donor nation with informal access to the host nation.

Virtually every form of United States assistance to a nation now offers a means of informal access of one kind or another. Public Law 480, for example, provides for shipping surplus food abroad. The recipient government then sells this food on the local market and deposits the local currency proceeds to the account of the United States. The expenditure of these funds, often totaling more than $500 million annually, is jointly negotiated by the United States and the recipient government. This is an adaptation of the Marshall Plan counterpart scheme but with greater formal control by the

United States than previously. One-fifth of the local currency thus deposited is used for administrative expenses and two-fifths is expended in the form of grants. The remaining two-fifths take the form of loans that may be repaid in local currency. When the loans are repaid, the funds are available for further use. A revolving fund is thus established that allows the United States to make expenditures in the host country years after the initial shipment of surplus food has been consumed.

The Development Loan Fund provides another example. It was established by Congress in 1957 and is designed to make funds available when there is a need in a developing area that cannot be met from any other source. This enables the United States to influence developments within a country by making funds available for some purposes and not for others and by attaching "strings" to a loan—normally stipulations relating to the efficient use of assistance.

An understanding of the informal penetration aspect of foreign aid should make it easier for Americans to view this assistance in a balanced way. Individuals who have no difficulty perceiving that Soviet foreign aid is an instrument of informal Soviet influence often overlook the same feature of United States assistance when they weigh its benefits against its costs. When, in November, 1963, Cambodia decided that it no longer wished to receive the very modest amount of aid allotted to it, some 2,400 Americans (including women and children) had to pack up and leave. The size of the American contingent indicates the access potential of foreign aid. When it is recalled that aid has been extended to over one hundred countries, its value as an instrument of informal access becomes clear. Informal penetration is rarely the most important objective of foreign aid, but it is nevertheless a by-product that should not be lost sight of. It is one of the reasons that the United States can do things with foreign aid that it can do in no other way.

The Peace Corps, another instrument of informal access, was established in 1961 in order to use the good will, energies, and talents of young Americans in the underdeveloped areas. This program is a cross between technical assistance and cultural exchange. Its administrators have been willing to accept a fairly low level of technical competence, measured by normal technical assistance standards, in return for dedication, a willingness to learn the language of the host country, and an eagerness to live with its people. Despite some growing pains, the undertaking has been a success in terms of its contribution both to the developing nations and to the improvement of the United States image abroad.

The North Atlantic Treaty Organization offers an interesting example of informal access via a multinational organization. Even though NATO has not provided an integrated defense system for the participating nations, it has, nevertheless, gone a long way beyond the traditional reliance on completely independent national defense systems. Each member nation retains formal authority over its own forces and actions but makes its decisions in the light of the decisions of the other NATO powers. There is a mutual (though not necessarily equal) influence of members upon one another. Strategic policy is the product of continual intergovernmental exchanges, and the sharing of the financial burden for the common defense is also a subject of review and negotiation.

While all of the NATO members influence one another's decisions, the position of the United States during most of NATO's life has been paramount. Given the military and financial preponderance of the United States and the fact that its deterrent power was the first line of defense for the NATO nations, it could hardly be otherwise. Until Charles de Gaulle acceded to the French presidency, the United States had dominated the defense policies of its allies for over a decade. For example, America's allies do not even control the nuclear weapons on their own soil; they are controlled by Americans. And, on occasion, an ally might not even know how many and what kinds of nuclear weapons were there.[2] This is not to challenge the wisdom of these policies but simply to note that it is informal access with a vengeance. So accustomed have some Americans become to this degree of influence that when President de Gaulle rejects American wishes and pursues an independent policy, including the development of a national nuclear force, his action is not merely disapproved on policy grounds but is regarded as if independence were in itself wicked.

The informal access that the United States achieves through the medium of the broader international organizations also deserves mention. Whether it deliberately seeks it or not, the United States often gains informal access to national societies as a consequence of its membership in international organizations. These organizations have contributed greatly to raising the general level of informal access in the international system, as will be shown in a later chapter. If a country has a particularly powerful voice in the operation of such an organization, it will achieve indirect informal access to the countries the organization deals with, by virtue of its influence within that organization.

In the International Monetary Fund, for example, the voting arrangements, which are based upon the financial contribution of the participating members, give the United States a preponderant voice in decisions. Through this power, the United States achieves indirect, informal influence over the economic policies of member nations since the fund has a degree of influence, though restricted, over the economic policies of those member nations. To illustrate, during the late 1950's, the United States used its influence to see that loans made to Latin American nations by the fund were conditioned upon the pursuit of stringent anti-inflation policies. As the fund becomes more important with the passage of time, the informal influence that the United States derives from it will increase.

The Inter-American Development Bank was established in 1959 to make "hard" loans to the Latin American nations, that is, loans repayable in dollars. Because the United States provided such a large proportion of the bank's resources, it has, under the voting rules, a predominant voice in its decisions. The United States member, therefore, casts 40 per cent of the votes of the bank. The Inter-American Fund for Special Operations, which was set up in conjunction with the bank to deal with "soft" loans—loans repayable in local currency—operates in much the same way. Since all loans by the Special Operations Fund must be approved by a two-thirds vote, the 40 per cent vote of the United States gives it an absolute veto. Other examples falling into this pattern could be cited, such as the UN and the Organization of American States.

The programs of the United States Information Agency provide excellent examples of informal access. Among other things, the agency facilitates the circulation of American newspapers, magazines, and books, subsidizes the translation of American books, circulates American films of many kinds, and operates the official radio voice of the United States. The information program is designed to explain American purposes and actions to peoples in other lands, to depict American culture and life in a favorable light, to point out the common interests that may bind the United States and other countries, and to counter unfriendly or inaccurate propaganda. In addition to the official radio voice, there are unofficial ones, such as Radio Free Europe and Radio Liberation. "Ostensibly the financing and direction of these broadcasting services was almost wholly nongovernmental. Actually the government's covert role was important. . . ." [3] Beyond this, of course, there are covert propaganda and related activities carried on by the Central Intelligence Agency that contribute to the informal access enjoyed by the United States.

The cultural exchange programs of the United States provide clear examples of the pursuit of informal access. The Fulbright Act of 1946, the Smith-Mundt Act of 1948, and the Agricultural Trade and Development and Assistance Act of 1954 contributed much of the substance of the program, and the Fulbright-Hays Act of 1961 broadened it still further. As a result, every year thousands of Americans are abroad on government-sponsored exchange programs, and several thousand foreign leaders—legislators, journalists, broadcasters, lawyers, labor leaders, women, civic leaders, educators, and people with technical specialties—visit the United States as guests of the government. In 1962, for example, there were close to 60,000 students from 49 countries studying in the United States, and the number has increased every year during the past decade. In a recent year, as part of the military training program of the Defense Department, 28,000 foreign officers and men trained in the United States.[4] When these visitors return home, they will presumably understand the United States better and, at least some of them, may prove to be avenues by which various ideas can be introduced into their homelands.

In the face of so great an influx of visitors, one can ask who is penetrating whom. The answer is, of course, that cultural exchange normally involves two-way penetration. The United States may achieve quasi-governmental penetration when American citizens are abroad under its sponsorship or when it invites foreign leaders to the United States. By the same token, when foreign leaders are in the United States, they may achieve a degree of informal access to the American political or governmental process, and certainly, when American citizens return from an extended stay in another country, they are likely to be sympathetic to the interests and needs of that country. However, although each nation in an exchange program may, to an extent, penetrate the other, the extent may vary greatly. For example, after a period of years, the exchange program might result in the United States having significant access to the decision-making process in a small nation in Southeast Asia, but that nation might have only peripheral access to the decision-making process in the United States. Furthermore, while a given nation may have an exchange program only with the United States, the United States is engaged in that program and many other.

When it is said that foreign visitors may sometimes achieve access to the political and governmental system, it should be stressed that the type of contact referred to is informal rather than formal and official. These visitors are not formal representatives engaging in direct, government-to-government negotiations. Their position would be more akin to that of the registered lobbyist, whether American citizen or alien, who works in Washington for a foreign government or interest. He is not an official representative of a foreign government confronting American policy after it has been formulated and enunciated, but an agent trying to influence policy informally before it has taken final form.

The cultural exchange programs of the United States were a response to the Cold War and were defined largely in negative terms at the outset. Now, however, these programs serve broader purposes and contribute to the advancement of common knowledge and to the furtherance of mutual understanding among nations. The fact that they are justified before Congress on the more mundane grounds of national interest, and quite properly so, in no way subtracts from the importance of their broader role. This is only one of a number of examples that could be cited in which a program undertaken on a defensive and restricted basis has acquired positive functions reaching far beyond the initial purpose of the country initiating the program. The Marshall Plan and Point IV both involve elements of this.

An important new example of informal support is military civic action. The interest in civic action grew out of efforts to cope with guerilla activities. If the support of the people of an area is indeed essential to the success of a guerilla movement, then denying this support to the guerilla forces is quite as important as winning combat actions against them. How does one deny support to a guerilla movement? Win that support for the established government!

Military civic action has been defined as:

> The use of preponderantly indigenous military forces on projects useful to the local population at all levels in fields such as education, training, public works, agriculture, transportation, communications, health, sanitation and others contributing to economic and social development, which would also serve to improve the standing of the military forces with the populations.[5]

The central idea involves the use of the skills of indigenous military forces to improve the social, political, and economic conditions of a people, and thus to win popular support. The skills of a military force—civil engineering, administration, communications, health, and sanitation—plus its organized, disciplined manpower, are elements needed by a developing nation. A force that can build roads for military purposes can build roads for civilian purposes. Similarly, a force that can build barracks for military use can build schools and other buildings for civilian use.

Civic action programs have been developed in a number of countries including those faced with guerilla activity, those threatened with insurgency, and those that are simply facing the problems of development. Thus, for example, in Guatemala, a United States Army unit aided the Guatemalan army in building irrigation facilities, purifying water, and in improving roads. In Ethiopia, American military advisers worked with the Ethiopian armed forces in building schools, drilling wells, and clearing roads. In Korea, during the ten years from 1953 to 1963, AFAK (Armed Forces Assistance to Korea) completed 4,537 projects, including the construction of schools, churches, orphanages, civic buildings, and bridges.[6] Whether the United States Army develops its own capabilities in this field, as in South Vietnam, or acts in a purely advisory capacity, it is still using a new technique of informal penetration to supplement those already used.

> In our instruction, writing, lectures and discussions concerning civic action we should point out that when the United States responds to a request for help in combatting insurgency, we offer the country concerned a variety of plans designed to promote its national integrity, its internal stability, and its freedom. Among these are economic aid administered primarily by AID; military assistance through the Department of Defense; selective education and training by people of the Peace Corps; political support under the direction of the Department of State; help in informational and psychological operations by the U.S. Information Agency.[7]

In countries with military civic action programs, indigenous military forces are being used to make over the nation—and the United States Army is helping with the remodeling. This is not said in the spirit of criticism. Civic action is an excellent way to use available manpower and skills and should probably be a part of any counterinsurgency program. It should also be considered by developing nations that are *not* faced with insurgency problems. The point to note, however, is that civic action makes the United States Army an instrument of conscious social change in foreign nations. General George H. Decker, former Army Chief of Staff, put it succinctly:

> We believe that the civic action program is not only essential in preventing and defeating active insurgency but we hold a program to be an invaluable asset in building a stronger social and economic framework for our countries.[8]

Another point worth noting about this example is the way in which the army, in order to achieve the relatively limited goal of crushing guerilla activity, has gradually been drawn into an effort to shape the social, political, and economic life of a country. The pattern is often seen. When American officials were trying to improve the resistance of South Vietnam to Communist guerilla activity, they came to realize that the problem could not be dealt with on a purely military level. The prospect of victory depended on strengthening the Diem regime by generating political support for it. To achieve these broader objectives, a variety of programs was developed—reorganization of the police force, plans for social reform, the preparation of an anti-inflation program, improved treatment of religious minorities, determining the composition of the import program, and so on. Each problem is related directly or indirectly to every other problem, and it appears fruitless to attack any one of them without doing something about the related problems at the same time. American officials thus find themselves drawn into one sector after another of the life of the host nation, even though intentions at the outset were modest. Starting with a limited objective in South Vietnam, the United States ended up providing guidance to the South Vietnamese government on virtually all significant aspects of its national life. When American officials concluded that the Diem regime would not institute needed reforms and hence would never win popular support, the United States government withdrew its protection and informal support, and the Diem regime was soon toppled.

The tendency for assistance to broaden out into additional fields is, of course, seen in the economic realm as well. The logic is much the same as that which has led American officials to be discontented when United States resources are devoted to uncoordinated local projects or to but a single problem in a country. If aid is to have a lasting effect on the economy of a developing country, there has to be improvement in the manner in which a variety of activities are planned, financed, and engineered. Furthermore, unless several problems are attacked simultaneously, the results will often be negligible and the resources wasted. As American officials convince officials of the host nation of this, there will be increased interest in central planning. Since the officials of the host nation do not normally possess the skill to undertake the planned use of national resources, Americans soon find themselves assisting in the actual planning as well as giving instructions in planning techniques. By a perfectly natural evolution, then, the host government finds itself involved in central planning, and American officials find themselves reshaping the economic life of the country. This informal penetration by Americans is not necessarily the result of a deliberate effort to extend the influence of the United States. It derives from efforts by Americans to help others solve their problems and from the realization by technicians that progress will be more rapid if problems are tackled simultaneously and on a coordinated basis.

The concern of economic aid officials may not be confined to the economy of the host country. Indeed, if their analysis is sufficiently thoroughgoing, it probably should not be so confined. American officials do not want their efforts wasted and hence want to be sure that the right economic decisions are made. The only way to make certain of this is to see to it that the right decision-makers are in office, which implies intervention in the political process. It would be anguishing for aid officials to stand by idly and watch men come to office who would undo the work of years. Whether the aid is economic, technical, or military, the donor nation often finds it difficult to avoid being drawn into the political arena.

American aid administrators gravitate toward the political realm because that is where the critical decisions are made. The success or failure of a given program is likely, therefore, to hinge on the political conditions that exist in the host country. It is an easy step from this realization to the conclusion that American officials ought to take steps informally (perhaps through the medium of CIA) to bring about political conditions that would be compatible with the program they favor. Informal American efforts in support of Magsaysay prior to the Philippine elections of 1953 illustrate the problem:

> Gradually, moreover, the increasing involvement of Americans aroused by a sense of urgency in the frustrating quest for solutions to these problems led them to the consciousness of a need for, and finally to a sense of responsibility for, a creative solution of a third set of problems: those of political leadership in the Philippine Republic. Americans found themselves involved in influencing the Philippine elections as a means of securing a leadership that would make their other proposed reforms effective. This remarkable development had not been premeditated far in advance, but was an outgrowth of the other more conventional cold-war programs of the islands.[9]

The political realm is more sensitive than the economic, and penetration in that quarter more easily provokes charges of intervention. When foreign advisers become concerned with campaigns, elections, and the press, it is easy for nationals of the host country to conclude that their sovereignty is being infringed. This is why many of the political activities of the United States are handled covertly by CIA. Often, however, the political activities that are needed, on the scale that they are needed, are not well adapted to covert execution. For that reason, American officials have begun to reach out for new ways of wielding political influence. Military civic action, as already noted, is one such way.

In recent years, governmental officials, in conjunction with non-governmental organizations, have been devoting attention to what has come to be called "political development." There is a growing realization that democratic institutions cannot be expected to arise spontaneously but must be nurtured. Democracy is no more "natural" than is autocracy or military rule. Indeed, it may be less natural in the sense that the prerequisites for a successful democracy are more numerous, complex, and difficult to achieve than are those for autocratic government. What are the processes by which political parties emerge in a developing society? How is the transition made from a single party to a multiparty system? How are leaders to be trained to toleration in a society that habitually relies on violence? What are the ways in which interest groups can be related to the governmental process? How is a society to be brought to the point at which it regards free and honest elections as a matter of prime importance? The deliberate construction of a democratic society is a complicated undertaking at best and is little understood by anyone at this juncture, including American administrators and social scientists who give advice on the subject. It is remarkably easy to mistake one's own historical patterns and culturally-induced political preferences for the laws of political development.

Some things can, of course, be done even on the basis of very imperfect knowledge. The AFL-CIO, for example, is performing a valuable service in training foreign labor leaders. One of the media through which it worked was the *Instituto de Educación Política* in Costa Rica, later called the *Instituto Internacional de Estudios Político-Sociales*. This institute is supported by parties of the democratic Left, such as *Acción Democrática* in Venezuela and the *Partido, Liberal* in Colombia, and by the AFL-CIO.[10] Juan Bosch, who was associated with the institute for a time, received substantial support from non-governmental organizations in his successful campaign for the presidency of the Dominican Republic in 1963. The Overseas Education Fund of the National League of Women Voters, to mention another example, has pioneered in training women from other countries for citizen activity and leadership. With the passage of time, there will no doubt be an increase in this type of activity both at governmental and non-governmental levels.

One of the most important instruments for informal attack and support used by the United States is the covert one. Until the abortive Cuban invasion, however, few Americans were aware of the secret political activities of the Central Intelligence Agency. To most of them, CIA was an intelligence agency and nothing more. The decision to engage in large-scale, covert political operations during *peacetime* was, in itself, a revolutionary innovation in American foreign policy. Polcies on lesser matters have been debated across the land for weeks and months, but, on this question, there was no debate in Congress, and the decision was closely held even within the executive branch. Thousands of persons were recruited, an organization was brought into being comparable in size to the Department of State, secret funds were made available in very generous amounts, and covert operations were begun around the world.

Since the decision to engage in covert activities on a global basis was never widely debated by elective officials, some persons have argued that the decision ought to be reexamined. After the Cuban invasion, for example, the Fellowship of Reconciliation of Nyack, New York, bought space in a number of papers to raise the moral issue:

> Americans have rightly condemned the Soviet Union for its aggressive intervention in the affairs of Hungary. How can we condone the participation of the United States, in violation of its own laws and treaty obligations, in the deliberate subversion of the Cuban government.
>
> Whatever you may now feel about Fidel Castro and his regime, do you not share with us a deep feeling of

shame that our government has pursued and is pursuing such a policy?

> We plead with our government to reverse its policies immediately. We plead with it to abandon a policy that would still be impolitic and immoral, whatever semblance of legality might be given it.[11]

Those who object to covert operations on moral grounds maintain that it is wrong for a government to say one thing and do another, to engage in bribery and the covert subsidy of foreign organizations, to claim to believe in self-government while organizing the violent overthrow of established governments. A nation that does these things, they say, makes a travesty of its claims to justice, morality, liberty, and self-determination and follows, instead, the doctrine that the end justifies the means.

Those of the opposite persuasion insist that the United States has no real choice. Fire must be fought with fire. Covert operations are an evil, perhaps, but a necessary evil. In the harsh world of international politics, they declare, morality, by itself, cannot be a sufficient guide to policy. The United States should press ahead knowing full well that some of its actions will not bear examination in the light of day.

As a practical matter, any debate at this time on the moral aspects of covert operations would come fifteen years too late. The policy has long been established, and it is extremely unlikely that pressure will build up for a change. If any development might have led to a review of the basic decision, it would have been a failure of the magnitude of the Cuban invasion. Instead, while there was a great deal of criticism of the planning, tactics, logistics, intelligence, and support aspects of the operation, criticism of its objective was rare. It was the failure of the effort, not the justifiability of the attempt in the first place, that drew criticism.

The basis on which moral objections to covert political warfare are overridden is the national interest. The case to be made for covert operations on the basis of national interest tends to be taken for granted, however, rather than examined seriously. Enthusiasts tend to exaggerate the capabilities of this instrument, complicating further an already difficult task of assessment. One of the factors that makes it difficult to assess covert activity, either before it is undertaken or afterwards, is the problem of weighing short-run interests against long-run interests. Typically, short-run gains, because they are more visible, concrete, and immediate than long-range considerations, tend to be given disproportionate weight.

In 1954, for example, when the Communist-dominated government of Arbenz was in power in Guatemala, the short-run advantage to be gained from its overthrow was clear. A covert operation was therefore planned, insurgent forces were armed, and the government was overthrown. Was the long-term interest of the United States served by this successful covert operation? The picture is less clear. For one thing, the Washington-sponsored government that came to power was short-lived. Furthermore, many Latin Americans, including those who disliked the Arbenz regime, were deeply troubled by the unilateral overthrow of a Latin American government by the United States. The coup was interpreted as a threat against other governments, and it outweighed a score of solemn declarations about respect for the sovereignty of other nations and the principle of the Good Neighbor. The incident has remained vivid in many Latin American minds despite the intervening years. The short-term interest of the United States pointed toward a coup, but the longer-range interest suggested patience and continued diplomatic and economic pressure.

The ill-starred Cuban invasion also illustrates the difficulty of discerning where the national interest lies in the covert field. At the time, the Kennedy Administration had concluded that Castro's continuation in office was contrary to American interests. It then had to decide whether to try to overthrow that government by covert means or to confine its actions to the political and economic sphere. How were the obvious short-term gains to be weighed against the principles of fair play, treaty obligations, the Good Neighbor policy, the principle of finding inter-American solutions for inter-American problems, and the predictable reactions of Latin American and other nations? Does a leading nation in the world have to be peculiarly alert to the danger of using *means* that may undermine the *ends* it purports to stand for? Does a nation seeking to offer political and moral leadership to others have to be peculiarly aware of its obligations and its reputation?

The decision was made to proceed with the invasion, and the debacle soon followed. The allies of the United States were stunned, leaders in neutral nations were denunciatory, criticism in Latin America was savage. Anti-American rioting and demonstrations broke out in Bogotá, Caracas, Montevideo, Mexico City, the Canal Zone, Buenos Aires, Guatemala City, Rio de Janiero, and La Paz. Since the invasion failed, it is easy to conclude that the entire operation was a mistake. If it had led to the overthrow of Castro, however, would that automatically have made it a wise undertaking?

Another factor to be weighed when a nation is considering covert political operations is whether the security of those operations can be maintained. If its ability to maintain secrecy is doubtful, it will be well advised to approach covert operations with caution. The U-2 incident provides an example of what may happen when a secret operation—in this case an intelligence operation rather than a covert political operation—is exposed. For several years, periodic high-altitude flights over the Soviet Union had been completed without incident and with a very substantial intelligence yield. Then, on May Day of 1960, Francis Gary Powers and the remains of his aircraft fell into Soviet hands. What was a routine intelligence operation one moment was an international incident the next. There was acute embarrassment in Washington, since the United States government was caught not only in a flagrant violation of Soviet air space but in a series of deliberate lies as well. Norway and Pakistan, which had cooperated with the United States in the overflights, were subjected to crude Russian military threats. Khrushchev used the incident to wreck the summit meeting and to force cancellation of President Eisenhower's visit to the Soviet Union. It strengthened the hand of those in China and the Soviet Union who felt that the Soviet government should pursue a more intractable policy toward the West. Furthermore, it jeopardized the signing of the Japanese-American Treaty, touched off rioting in Japan that led to the humiliating last-moment cancellation of President Eisenhower's visit to Japan, and contributed to the fall of the Kishi government. The reputation of the United States thus suffered serious injury from the incident.

To be sure, it is possible that plans will not go astray and that an operation will remain secret. However, the record of the United States in security matters does not generate unlimited confidence. As covert operations increase in number, scope, and complexity, the difficulty of maintaining security increases rapidly. With a really large operation, anything like complete secrecy becomes a chimera, save under wartime conditions.

The otherthrow of the Arbenz regime in Guatemala is regarded as one of the more successful United States covert efforts, yet the imprint of the United States was all over the operation.[12] Indeed, the Guatemalan affair can be termed "covert" only in the spirit of charity. Newspapers were frank in reporting the role of the United States, and *The New York Times Magazine* soon carried an article by Flora Lewis, in ecstatic prose, describing the exploits of "Ambassador Extraordinary: John Peurifoy."

Thinly curtained from the full spotlight by Washington's effort not to appear directly involved in the Guatemalan revolution, his [Ambassador Peurifoy's] role was at all times important. At some moments it was probably decisive.[13]

Miss Lewis goes on to describe how the ambassador, wearing his own revolver in a shoulder holster, made decisions instantly "sometimes in a setting of well-oiled tommy guns." However, the rule book says that, when an uprising of this kind takes place, the ambassador of the country that organized it should be miles from the scene of the operation. Yet, the ambassador of the United States was up to his ears in the whole affair. One may wonder why the president did not simply order in the United States Marines and have done with it.

The Cuban invasion, including the security aspects of the operation, is a horror story from start to finish. The United States is an open society, its citizens unused to secrecy and its press energetic and enterprising. In view of this, the decision to use parts of the United States mainland as one of the bases for the organization of a large-scale, covert, paramilitary operation is a strange one. Since the operation had an important political dimension and would necessarily raise powerful passions in the Cuban *émigré* population in Miami, the decision seems even stranger.[14]

An observant newspaper reader could hardly have failed to see evidence of the preparations months before the invasion. There were hints in the press about training exercises in Florida, and the *Saturday Evening Post* prepared an illustrated article on the subject that it withheld until after the invasion because it would have embarrassed American authorities. On January 10, 1961, *The New York Times* carried a front page story about the "secret" preparations in Guatemala:

US HELPS FOES OF CASTRO
AT SECRET GUATEMALA BASE

Retalhuleu, Guatemala, January 9—
This area is the focal point of Guatemala's military preparations for what Guatemalans consider will be an almost inevitable clash with Cuba.

There is intensive daily air training here from a partly hidden airfield. In the Cordillera foothills a few miles back from the Pacific, commando-like forces are being drilled in guerilla warfare tactics by foreign personnel, mostly from the United States.

The United States is assisting this effort not only in personnel but in material and the construction of ground and air facilities.

Guatemalan authorities from President Miguel Ydigoras Fuentes down insist that the military effort is designed to meet an assault, expected almost any day, from Cuba.

Opponents to the Ydigoras Administration have insisted that the preparations are for an offensive against Cuba and that it is being planned and directed, and to a great extent paid for, by the United States.

The United States Embassy is maintaining complete silence on the subject. Guatemalan authorities will speak only guardedly about it . . .

After the invasion failure, President Kennedy acknowledged that ". . . details of this nation's covert preparations to counter the enemy's covert operations have been available to every newspaper reader, friend and foe alike . . ." [15]

The question of the national interest is complicated still further if one considers the implications of covert operations for the conduct of foreign policy in a democracy. There are two aspects of the problem that should be noted. First, there is the problem of how there can be meaningful participation in the decision-making process by the Congress and by interested organizations and individuals if a vast web of governmental activities must remain hidden for security reasons. It is difficult at best to conduct foreign policy in a democracy, and the advent of global political operations of a secret nature compounds the problem. It raises the question of whether there is any limit to the extent and kind of secrecy that a nation can tolerate before the democratic process itself begins to be impaired.

The second problem concerns the difficulty of extending responsible government to the realm of covert operations. When blunders are made in other policy areas there are Congressional investigations, protests by interested groups, excited editorials, and possibly reprisal at the polls. The activities of CIA are so sensitive, however, that they cannot be discussed publicly or even mentioned, cannot be debated widely in Congress, and are closely held even within the executive branch. Except in the rare case of a failure that is so big it cannot be hidden—again the Cuban example—darkness and silence are the rule. The area of activity that is involved, furthermore, is one of great importance to the nation. Covert operations can not only create the possibility of war; they also have explosive possibilities for the disruption of American relations with friendly and neutral nations. The reaction can easily be imagined if it became widely known in an allied nation, or a nation whose friendship the United States was wooing, that Washington had for several years been secretly subsidizing selected newspapers, labor unions, non-governmental organizations, or political parties within its borders. Since covert operations are playing a growing role in the foreign operations of the United States, this means that the sphere of activity insulated from the political process is becoming progressively larger with the passage of time. Is it appropriate that a large and wealthy agency should conduct secret political and paramilitary operations in nations all over the world—friendly, unfriendly, and neutral—without the best provisions for oversight and checking that a democratic society can devise?

To be sure, when all is said and done, the interest of the United States dictates the continuation of covert activities as long as the nation is engaged in severe informal conflict with the Soviet Union and Communist China. These operations should be screened more closely and perceptively in the future, however, than they have been in the past.

A deliberate effort should be made to weigh all aspects of the national interest and not to give disproportionate weight to immediate interests simply because they are more immediate and obvious. Finally, improved means must be developed for genuine oversight of covert operations by committees of Congress. Perfunctory, periodic "briefing" of a few individuals is not satisfactory. In one of its forms, this oversight might involve a more careful scrutiny of the expenditure of funds by CIA. It is an interesting anomaly that the Congress, which has exhibited a lively interest in the activities, policies, and expenditures of the Department of State over the years, should be content to do little more than write a blank check to the CIA year after year. Indeed, since the bulk of CIA funds are hidden in the appropriations of other departments and agencies, only a handful of Congressmen know what the total CIA appropriation figure is or when they are actually approving funds for CIA use. In a letter to Senator Mansfield in March, 1959, C. P. Cabell, then Acting Director of the CIA wrote: "The CIA appropriation figure is very tightly held and is known to not more than five or six members in each house." [16]

One of the most useful instruments for informal access yet developed in the Western Hemisphere is, of course, the Alliance for Progress. With the Alliance, American administrators found an approach that, for the first time, allowed a frank and candid expression of American interest in the political, social, and economic development of other nations. Its significance in the evolution of American thinking about informal influence and support can scarcely be exaggerated. For that reason, and because its advent illustrates so well the ambiguous nature of the American foreign policy tradition, it is worth discussing its emergence at some length.

Near the turn of the century, the practice of United States intervention in Latin American affairs was well established. Some seventy examples of such intervention can be listed.[17] Most, but not all, of these involved formal rather than informal intervention. For example, when the French abandoned their canal-building project in Panama, the United States tried to buy the French assets via a treaty with Colombia. However, the Colombian Senate, dissatisfied with its terms and angered by United States pressure, rejected the treaty. In a rapid series of events following this rejection, Panama revolted and received American recognition. Within fifteen days, another treaty was signed with the new Panamanian government giving the United States exclusive rights to a strip of land ten miles wide across the isthmus. In the meantime, American warships in the area had deterred Colombian troops from suppressing the rebellion. Later Theodore Roosevelt could remark, "I took the canal." The Roosevelt Corollary to the Monroe Doctrine, developed in 1905, arrogated policing responsibilities in the Western Hemisphere to the United States and provided further rationalization for United States intervention in Latin American affairs when it felt the necessity.

With the passage of years, however, and a decline in the need of the United States to intervene in Latin America, the practice of intervention came to be regarded as morally reprehensible. For a generation, textbooks in American history have treated the "Big Stick" era as one of the more shameful episodes in the national past. The development of the Good Neighbor policy under Franklin Roosevelt can be interpreted, in part, as an effort by the United States to atone for its earlier transgressions.

To give support to the President's enunciation of the Good Neighbor policy in the 1933 inaugural address, the United States signed and ratified the Convention on the Rights and Duties of States drawn up at the Montevideo Conference in 1933. The United States was, in effect, taking the pledge when it agreed to Article IV, which reads, "No state has the right to intervene in the internal or external affairs of another." Next, the Platt Amendment, which had given the United States the right to intervene in Cuba, was abrogated in 1934. Then, in 1936, the Declaration of Principles of Inter-American Solidarity and Cooperation drawn up in Buenos Aires and accepted by the United States stated that "Intervention by one state in the internal or external affairs of another state is condemned." These same sentiments were echoed in the 1938 Declaration of Lima and received a strong restatement in the Charter of the Organization of American States signed at Bogotá in 1948.

The doctrine of non-intervention is based on the hope that nations might live and let live; and it is admirable in spirit. However, it assumes a world in which nations have mutual respect for each other's territorial integrity and in which they are set apart in space and do not interact or interpenetrate significantly. Non-intervention assumes, in short, the lost world of impenetrable nation-states. And it also assumes a world in which there are no unusually powerful countries. When a nation is powerful, the question is not *whether* it will affect its neighbors but only *how* it will affect them. It intervenes in the affairs of others simply by being powerful. Its military policies and alliance policies will affect the security calculations of scores of nations, both those that are allied with it and those that are not. Its trading policies and its fiscal and monetary decisions will have repercussions around the world. A great nation, therefore, cannot avoid influencing other nations, and this influence will often appear to them as interference.

Such a nation cannot attempt to provide positive leadership and, at the same time, avoid intervention, for the very means by which it exercises its leadership constitute interference. The United States cannot, therefore, help the emerging nations to modernize without intervening in their affairs. Its help *is* intervention. Nor can it exercise leadership in matters of NATO policy without trying to guide and press other nations to its way of thinking, for leadership consists of such guidance and pressure.

Here, then, were American administrators responsible for dealing with the Latin American countries. They were supposed to take their policy guidance from the series of broad statements celebrating the principle of non-intervention, yet they were faced with a host of concrete problems that pointed toward programs in conflict with the spirit and letter of the nation's international commitments. The response of American policy-makers to the conflict between formal doctrine on the one hand and practical needs on the other took several forms. One response was to overlook the role the United States was playing in the affairs of others. For example, the fact that the United States was not merely aiding the European nations during the European Recovery Program but was actively engaged in trying to remodel many of their economic institutions and processes received little comment at the time.

A somewhat similar method of obscuring the conflict between doctrine and behavior lay in the translation of all issues of importance—political, social, and economic—into a neutral terminology that allowed them to be dealt with on a limited, technical basis. Programs that would remake the way of life of the country to which they were directed were debated as if the real problem were that of achieving administrative "efficiency." Matters relating to developmental aid, despite their nation-shaping impact, were studiously treated as merely "economic," and hence as "non-political." The emphasis was on the "technical" in technical assistance. The image presented was that of a handful of American soil experts teaching plowing techniques and the advantages of crop rotation. In fact, those "technical" activities have included advice on legislation, legal procedures, economic policy, property ownership, human rights, social organization, labor relations, social welfare, fiscal and monetary policy, production and distribution systems, the role of non-governmental organizations, the development of political parties, and electoral procedures. As the process of modernization picks up momentum in an emerging nation, scarcely any compartment of the national life is left untouched. Agriculture, industry, public administration, politics, education, religion, family, social relations, worker-employer relations—all will feel the impact of change. In giving aid, therefore, a donor country will necessarily set a train of events in motion, whether it wishes to or not, and the net result will be to change the society receiving the aid. A nation that is ambivalent about intervention will find it difficult to acknowledge this, however.

It is hard for men and agencies to perform tasks well when their ideology suggests that these tasks should not be performed at all. The doctrine of non-intervention has served to hamper the development of effective aid administration, to slow the evolution of ideas and techniques for dealing with the problems of development, and it has stood in the way of a candid recognition by American officials of what they have, in fact, been doing for two decades.

Before the energies and talents of American officials could be freed to operate in a creative and imaginative way, the doctrine of non-intervention had to be replaced by a different doctrine, one that taught that intervention might be a positive good. With the Alliance for Progress, that new doctrine was promulgated. Intervention was no longer an evil but a responsibility that the United States was forced to assume, if reluctantly and tardily. "We in the United States have made many mistakes in our relations with Latin America," President Kennedy told an audience in Bogotá in 1961. "We have not always understood the magnitude of your problems, or accepted our share of responsibility for the welfare of the Hemisphere." [18]

No longer was aid to be treated as purely non-political and "technical." Instead, along with the tremendous program of development[19] outlined by the Charter of Punta del Este has come explicit recognition that aid can be effective only if it is accompanied by major social, political, and economic reforms in recipient countries. "These social reforms are at the heart of the Alliance for Progress," President Kennedy said in his Bogotá address. "They are the precondition to economic modernization. . . . We ask that substantial and steady progress toward reform accompany the effort to develop the economies of the American nations."

The Alliance has thrust the United States deeply into the affairs of the Latin American nations. For one thing, the United States has committed itself to playing a major role in financing Alliance activities. Furthermore, it has, at present, a virtual monopoly, in this hemisphere, of men trained to tackle the tasks envisioned by the Alliance. American officials will give advice to host nations on scores of matters, including some that are of immediate and substantial importance. Moreover, they will have working relationships with employers' organizations, labor representatives, planning groups, legislatives groups, interest organizations, and political parties.

The Charter of Punta del Este signifies the demise of non-intervention as a guiding principle in American foreign policy and the birth of a philosophy of purposeful, unashamed involvement in the affairs of other nations. If this appears to be a naked expression of American self-interest, it should be stressed that there is often mutuality of purpose between the penetrating nation and the host nation. Informal penetration includes measures for both informal attack and informal support. The Alliance for Progress involves United States intervention in Latin American affairs, but it is an intervention that was deliberately sought by the Latin American nations. The view of the Eisenhower Administration that Latin American nations should face up to their own problems and not wait for the United States to solve them was thoroughly in keeping with the hands-off posture associated with the Good Neighbor policy, but it did not meet the needs of Latin America. For years, spokesmen for these nations had complained that the United States had paid too much attention to Western Europe and too little to problems of the Western Hemisphere. Their plea to the United States for leadership in dealing with these problems was, necessarily, a plea for United States intervention. The role of the United States in the Alliance is, then, interventionist and will certainly interfere with the "sovereignty" of those nations. The alternative was to respect their sovereignty *against their wishes,* and refuse to help them. The influence of the United States in the Alliance is, therefore, mutually desired and is of an un-sinister nature. It should also be noted that while the Alliance gives the United States access to the planning processes of Latin American nations it also gives the governments of these countries access to one another's planning processes. Country programs must be submitted to the scrutiny of committees composed of representatives of several Alliance nations. This procedure, if cumbersome, is nevertheless of historic significance.

The objective of the Alliance is nothing less than the revolutionizing of a continent, and, whether it succeeds or not, it represents a turning point in United States thinking about its relations with other nations. The implications of the Alliance, and other examples of United States intervention, have not been fully grasped, however, either in Washington or in foreign capitals.

A nation that is to play a leading role in world affairs

has no alternative but to set aside, or at least modify, the principle of non-intervention. A doctrinal adherence to non-intervention by the United States in today's world would be an invitation to disaster—disaster not only for the United States but for the nations that depend upon its strength and leadership. It is in the interests of these nations that the United States forsake non-intervention. This is not to suggest, of course, that host nations are unambivalent in their acceptance of American intervention. Quite the contrary. The ideal of non-intervention retains a great deal of appeal, and many nations are a long way from abandoning it as a basis for assessing American foreign policy, even though their interests would suffer grievously if the United States did, in fact, adhere to it. It may be a triumph for a government when it receives a substantial grant from Washington, but that same government may also have to fight a running battle internally to avoid being labeled a tool of the United States because it negotiated the grant. Thus, although foreign governments want American aid, they have decidedly mixed feelings about the increase in American influence that tends to accompany it. They ask for aid—and simultaneously applaud the doctrine of non-intervention.

This ambivalence is thoroughly understandable and indicates that ideas are in the process of change. The host nations do not find it easy to give up their attachment to the doctrine of non-intervention because it represents a summation, an embodiment, of their ideas on the relationship that should obtain between great powers and smaller nations. To forsake non-intervention, they fear, would be to legitimize intervention. An ambivalence of a complementary kind can be found in the United States, and it, too, signifies that ideas are in transition. If foreign governments are not always certain that American assistance is worth the cost, in terms of unavoidable restrictions on their freedom of action, some people in the United States question whether the returns from intervention are worth either the psychological or dollar costs. Host nations fear that the United States may be inclined to intervene unduly if the non-intervention barrier is lowered; and many Americans feel that the United States may be drawn into an infinite number of costly and endless interventions around the world. Rejection of unconditional non-intervention, however, does not imply—as seems to be feared—acceptance of a doctrine of unconditional *intervention*. Such a doctrine would not be in accordance with the interests and capabilities of the United States, and certainly other nations would find repugnant a doctrine that appeared to teach that the United States could properly intervene anywhere, at any time, in any manner it deemed fit.

The doctrinal evolution appears to be moving in a different direction. Both the United States and host nations show signs of recognizing, slowly and painfully, that the political, economic, and military realities of the world situation have made the principle of non-intervention obsolete. They appear to be in the process of grasping two aspects of what is a single truth: (1) The United States must realize that it will need to devote a substantial portion of its energies and resources to international leadership for the indefinite future. (2) The nations associated with the United States must understand that, for a variety of reasons, the acceptance of American leadership and assistance is likely to entail acceptance of a higher degree of foreign intervention than they have known in the past. If the United States must face up to the assumption of heavy international burdens, as its friends abroad assure it that it must, then the nations whose burdens it is helping to bear must learn to be responsible and tolerant in accepting assistance. For both parties, the lesson is a dual one and each finds it easier to accept that part of the lesson that applies most directly to the other. If either party is unable to accept the substance of the lesson, however, and acts accordingly, both may suffer heavy consequences.

To facilitate the learning of this lesson, it might be helpful to fashion a doctrine of "conditional intervention" (or, perhaps more palatably, "conditional non-intervention"). The emergence of a doctrine of this kind would direct attention away from the question of whether intervention is good or bad per se and toward the consideration of the *conditions* under which it may be mutually beneficial and acceptable, the forms that it might legitimately take, and the safeguards that might surround it. The concept of conditional intervention would provide a framework within which meaningful discussion and bargaining could take place since it would be based on an acceptance of the need for both intervention *and* restraints and safeguards. It might also provide a basis on which the United States and associated nations could develop an agreed code of behavior since it would recognize as legitimate the desire of the United States to wield influence in a country receiving its aid and also the desire of the host government to circumscribe the role of the United States in certain respects. At the outset the formulation of such a code would require little more than an effort to make explicit the thinking that underlies a great many present practices.

The existence of agreed guidelines would make it easier for the United States to exercise its power in a consistent and responsible way, and it would ease the minds of other governments. The CIA, for example, makes leaders in many countries uneasy. They cannot forget Guatemala, Iran, Cuba, the role of CIA in South Vietnam, and rumors of other exploits. There is room here for negotiation and for a better understanding. If there were guidelines governing intervention, Americans would find it easier to know when to be shamefaced and when not. Americans should be sensitive, not to the charge that the United States has intervened abroad, but to the charge that it has intervened unnecessarily, or unwisely, or ineffectively, or for the wrong purposes, or in disregard of a previous understanding, or that it *failed* to intervene when it should have.

Despite its lack of previous experience in informal penetration and its ambivalence about intervening in the affairs of others, the United States has learned its lessons comparatively well and quickly since World War II. As it has turned its attention, resources, and ingenuity to the task of developing informal influence, its capacity to affect the domestic and foreign policy decisions of other countries has grown rapidly. American administrators have learned a great deal during the past two decades, but the art of informal penetration will, no doubt, remain an imperfect one. The results achieved, therefore, will frequently not be those that are sought.

On the whole, the United States has proceeded by responding to immediate problems—often improvising brilliantly—rather than by achieving an understanding of the overall situation. Given the economic orientation of the nation, it was perhaps to be expected that the United States should innovate more effectively in the economic realm than in the political. After all, Americans are accustomed to assume that the source of a problem—almost any problem—must be economic and that its solution must also be economic. This has slowed American understanding of the complexity of social change and of the need for a frank recognition of the political context in which social and economic change takes place.

The broad purposes behind American intervention have been respectable even if individual examples have been ill-conceived and ill-executed. An inspection of its behavior reveals that the United States has felt a sense of reponsibility for trying to hold together the fabric of the international order. However remote geographically a dispute or problem may be, the United States has tended to feel that it must do what it can to improve the situation. The Soviet Union and Communist China, whether operating independently or together, do not start from the assumption that it is desirable to abate tension and settle problems. Disputes are to be settled and stability is to be promoted only when it serves a purpose. For the rest, they are content to fish in troubled waters. Since it is far easier to stir up troubles on this vexed planet than it is to set them at rest, irresponsible nations have a distinct advantage. The responsible nations, on the other hand, must forever bustle about trying to patch up this difficulty, redress that grievance, and prevent things from coming apart at the seams. It is a critically important task, but one that is expensive, little understood by others, wearying, and almost impossible to accomplish. If, over the years, the Soviet Union should come to think and act more as a responsible status quo power, the task, though still difficult, would be noticeably eased.

Notes

1 *Foreign Affairs,* July, 1947, pp. 566-582.

2 Alistair Buchan, *NATO in the 1960's,* revised edition (New York: Praeger, 1963), p. 67.

3 H. Bradford Westerfield, *The Instruments of America's Foreign Policy* (New York: Crowell, 1963), pp. 247-248.

4 Philip H. Coombs, "The Past and Future in Perspective," in *Cultural Affairs and Foreign Relations,* Robert Blum, editor (New York: Prentice-Hall, 1963), p. 164.

5 Quoted in Major General William B. Rosson, "Understanding Civic Action," *Army,* July, 1963, p. 47.

6 Jack Raymond, *Power at the Pentagon* (New York: Harper and Row, 1964), p. 115.

7 Major General William B. Rosson, "Understanding Civic Action," *Army,* July, 1963, p. 47.

8 Quoted in Colonel Robert H. Slover, "This Is Military Civic Action," *Army,* July, 1963, p. 48.

9 H. Bradford Westerfield, *The Instruments of America's Foreign Policy* (New York: Crowell, 1963), pp. 409-410.

[10] It has also been suggested that CIA funds were involved.

[11] *New York Times,* April 25, 1961.

[12] For an interesting discussion see Philip B. Taylor, "The Guatemalan Affair, a Critique of United States Policy," *The American Political Science Review,* L (September, 1956), 787-806.

[13] *New York Times Magazine,* July 18, 1954.

[14] These training activities in Florida involved a violation of the neutrality legislation that makes it a crime for anyone to aid, prepare, or participate in a military expedition from the United States against a foreign state with which this country is at peace. Since the Federal Bureau of Investigation had responsibility for prosecuting violators of the Neutrality Act and had, in fact, prosecuted Cuban nationals who were supporting Batista and others supporting Castro, a rather delicate situation was created. One federal agency, the CIA, was financing and directing activities that another federal agency was supposed to prosecute.

[15] *New York Times,* April 28, 1961.

[16] *Congressional Record,* March 10, 1959, p. 281.

[17] *Congressional Digest,* November, 1962, pp. 261-262.

[18] Presidential Address at San Carlos Palace, Bogotá, Colombia, December 17, 1961, reprinted in *President Kennedy Speaks on the Alliance for Progress* (Washington: Agency for International Development, Department of State, 1962), p. 18.

[19] The scope of the reforms sought in the Charter of Punta del Este is overwhelming:

To improve and strengthen democratic institutions . . .

To accelerate economic and social development . . .

To carry out urban and rural housing programs . . .

To encourage . . . programs of comprehensive agrarian reforms . . .

To assure fair wages and satisfactory working conditions . . .

To wipe out illiteracy . . . and to provide broader facilities on a vast scale for secondary and technical training and for higher education.

To press forward with programs of health and sanitation . . .

To reform tax laws . . . and to redistribute the national income in order to benefit those who are most in need, while, at the same time, promoting savings and investment and reinvestment of capital.

To maintain monetary and fiscal policies which, while avoiding disastrous effects of inflation and deflation, will protect the purchasing power of the many, guarantee the greatest possible price stability, and form an adequate basis for economic development.

To stimulate private enterprise . . .

To find a quick and lasting solution to the grave problems created by excessive price fluctuations in the basic exports of Latin American countries . . .

To accelerate the integration of Latin America so as to stimulate the economic and social development of the continent.

Taken from the Declaration to the Peoples of America, Punta del Este, Uruguay, August 17, 1961. Reprinted in *Alliance for Progress* (Washington: the Pan American Union, 1961), pp. 3-4.

CHAPTER IV

Disloyalty, Ideology, and Informal Access

The mass production of treason and disloyalty has been a specialty of the twentieth century, and the history of the century cannot be understood without reference to it. Austrians, Czechs, Norwegians, Frenchmen, Albanians, Bulgars, Rumanians, Cubans, Chinese, Russians, Americans—men and women of several score nations —have aided and abetted the designs of foreign powers against their homelands. The names of the disloyal can be extended indefinitely: Pierre Laval, Marshal Petain, Vidkun Quisling, Knut Hamsun, Conrad Henlein, Arthur von Seyss-Inquart, Bruno Pontecorvo, William Joyce, Klaus Fuchs, Alan Nunn May, Guy Burgess and Donald McLean, John Amery, Herman Rauschning, Otto Strasser, Admiral Canaris, Karl Friedrich Goerdeler, Ulrich von Hassel, General Ludwig Beck, Klaus von Stauffenberg, Richard Sorge, General Vlasov, and Igor Gouzenko.

The list of disloyal Americans is long, and neither Right nor Left has a monopoly of the membership: Alger Hiss, David Greenglass, Ethel and Julius Rosenberg, Whittaker Chambers, Elizabeth Bentley, Judith Coplon, William Martin and Vernon Mitchell, Ezra Pound, Mildred (Axis Sally) Gillars, Eva (Tokyo Rose) Toguri, and Robert Best, to mention a few.

Disloyalty is not restricted to a handful of psychological oddities. For every one of the preceding names, there are dozens or even hundreds less well-known. Fritz Kuhn had the ranks of the German-American Bund behind him. Behind General Vlasov, there was the Russian Army of Liberation; behind Seyss-Inquart were the Austrian Nazis; behind Laval, the defeatist and pro-Nazi elements in France. Associated with Von Stauffenberg in the July 20 plot on Hitler's life were the men in "Rote Kapelle" and the Kreisau Circle. During the 1961 crisis over Algerian independence, preparations were made in France to meet an expected mass attack on the homeland by discontented French paratroopers based in North Africa.

It is no exaggeration to speak of the disloyalty of millions. In 1946, as part of the purge of collaborators in France, more than 500,000 men and women were arrested on suspicion of treason, and, of this number, 160,000 were brought to trial. According to an American estimate, 100,000 Frenchmen were killed as collaborationists after the liberation—more lives than France lost on the battlefield and in prison camps. In Belgium, there were 60,000 investigations of alleged collaboration and in Holland 130,000.[1] For Europeans, loyalty problems were not confined to distant and unlikely persons; they were an everyday occurrence. All strata of society were touched. Not only were deputies and governmental ministers torn by competing loyalties but villagers and farmers as well.

Before World War II and during its early stages, men watched one nation after another submit to Nazi pressures. The explanation usually offered for the conduct of these nations was that they were sick or decayed. As more and more of them—including healthy ones—had to be placed on the sick roll, the tendency was to explain their behavior in terms of a general malaise. The quantitative increase in disloyalty certainly demands an explanation, but dismissing it as a symptom of global sickness does not help to pinpoint the nature of the problem.

The growth of treason and disloyalty has closely paralleled the growth of informal penetration in time and scale. This is no coincidence, for the two phenomena are causally related. The key to an understanding of the quantitative increase in disloyal behavior in the twentieth century lies in the development of informal penetration.

The purpose of many forms of informal attack and support is to change the attitudes and loyalties of the target population. Indeed, the success of a given technique is often measured in terms of the extent to which loyalties have been modified. The media used for informal penetration—radio, newspapers, journals, agitation, political parties, front groups, cultural exchanges, guerilla warfare—are deliberately chosen on the basis of their effectiveness in this respect. To say that there has been a vast increase in informal penetration activities during the past half-century is only another way of saying that the assault on men's loyalties is quantitatively far greater than it once was. Since the capacity of men to withstand this kind of attack has probably not changed significantly, the increased pressure on their allegiance must necessarily result in a greater incidence of disloyal behavior.

Achieving technical access is an indispensable first step for any informal penetration that aims at men's loyalties. The propaganda broadcast that reaches no ears, the leaflet that meets no eyes, the organization that has no members cannot possibly be successful. However, success requires substantive penetration as well. The message must not only be heard or read; it must strike a responsive chord. But the problems associated with substantive access are often more difficult than those connected with technical access. The bulk of this chapter, therefore, will be devoted to their exploration.

Too little is known about the psychology and sociology of disloyalty, and one of the reasons for this is that so little is known about loyalty. Yet it is almost impossible to imagine a man without loyalties. If an individual is not mentally ill, a web of attachments will bind him to family, community, neighborhood, state, nation, fraternal associations, union, and associates. His perceptions, his emotions, and his behavior will be largely organized in terms of this complex of loyalties.

An unreflective individual may have little awareness of the loyalties he feels. Even a reflective and articulate individual would be hard pressed to describe with precision his set of loyalties and the priorities he has established among them. Loyalties cannot be weighed and measured with nicety, for they interpenetrate and blend into one another and change over a period of time. If a man's loyalties are challenged, however, he is likely to discover their rough outlines soon enough.

Loyalty is an attitude, and as many factors influence its formation as influence any other attitude—fear, habit, education, reflection, perceptions, experience, age, example, affection. An individual's loyalties will be affected by his subconscious needs, by his wants and fears, and by the events taking place about him. Loyalty, in short, may be influenced by almost anything that happens in an individual's environment and by his response to what happens. Because so many factors can influence them, a man's loyalties are in a perpetual state of change. The changes that result may be as trivial as shifting from one brand of cigarettes to another or as profound as the transformation that overtook Saul on the road to Damascus. Since a man's behavior is organized in terms of his loyalties, shifts in these loyalties imply shifts in his behavior.

The evolution of a man's loyalties usually creates few political problems. He gives up checkers for chess, tennis for golf, devotes less time to his church and more to his lodge, less time to his mistress and more to his wife

—and no very great consequences follow. The change of loyalties is as natural as the change of the seasons. Suppose, however, that he now begins to give less time to the Democratic or Republican party and more to the Communist party. The process involved is fundamentally the same, but the state and one's fellow citizens will regard the shift quite differently, for loyalty to the nation is now involved.

Treason is not a sport of nature, unrelated to normal thinking and behavior and requiring unique tools for its analysis. Men withdraw loyalty from their nation by psychological processes that are similar to those by which other attitudes change. The consequences of their action may be more far-reaching in this case, but the psychology involved is not necessarily more complex.

> Patriotism, as an ordinary and commonplace social fact, must be regarded in ordinary and commonplace terms. This means that patriotism—and treason—must be analyzed as the products of social situations and of human reactions to those situations.[2]

Loyalty to the nation is not a "natural" and inescapable feeling. It is a learned response, and what men learn they can unlearn. Throughout history, men have given loyalty to, and withdrawn it from, all manner of chieftains, princes, popes, prime ministers, presidents, kings, emperors, cities, churches, empires, and parties. In the same way, they can give their loyalty to a nation—and they can withdraw it.

Over the years an individual learns the attitudes, values, and behavior patterns of a society. As he learns them and makes them his own, he is said to be socialized. Political socialization of an individual involves his acquisition of the political values of a society. The process of socialization usually takes place during the early decades of life, but it is sometimes belated. A scientist, for example, discovering the political realm for the first time in his middle age, can be as naive and untutored as a child.

Politically socialized people represent a pool of potential members for political groups in the society. If an individual's interest is great enough, he may become active in, say, the Democratic or Republican party. Suppose, however, that a young man does not follow the usual path of political socialization but instead becomes intrigued by an alien ideology. He may acquire a different set of values and attitudes and respond to a thoroughly different set of legitimacy symbols. He would be likely to acquire a new set of aversions, including aversion to his country, its leaders, and its policies. He has been politically socialized, but into an outlook shared by few of his compatriots. He, too, is ripe for political recruitment, but instead of becoming a Democrat or a Republican he may be recruited into the Communist party. The basic processes involved are, nevertheless, much the same, even though the net result may be quite different.

The difficult point is to understand *why* one man follows one course and another a quite different one. Human motivation is no more uniform in this area than in any other. The disloyalty of the determined idealist and that of the lost, anomic individual may be similar in outward form and yet be significantly different. Count Klaus von Stauffenberg carefully placing a bomb-laden briefcase at Hitler's feet and Lee Harvey Oswald huddled in the window of the Texas School Book Depository with rifle ready were both attempting political assassination, and each thought he was going to slay a tyrant. Yet one was in touch with reality and the other was not. To understand disloyalty, it is not enough to focus exclusively on the disloyal act itself or on the psychology of the individual. There must be a simultaneous examination of the total situation—the individual, the environment, his relation to that environment, and the significance of the disloyal act itself.

Loyalty and disloyalty depend on the way an individual perceives his environment and interacts with it.

There is room, therefore, for an almost infinite variety of patterns. Some people go through the process of political socialization and learn the appropriate rituals and behavior patterns without being deeply affected by the experience. Under trial they might easily be reasoned, argued, or frightened out of their attachments. Others, having gone through the same process of socialization, would be virtually unshakable in their loyalties and would scarcely recant if they were to be burned at the stake. One individual may be economically deprived but thoroughly loyal. Another may appear to have everything that life can offer and yet be disaffected. One may have little status and be content while another, highly placed, may be starved for greater position and recognition. Thus, although a man's loyalty may be strained if society does not provide him with minimal satisfactions, the kind of satisfactions he needs will depend on his personality and the nature of the society in which he finds himself.

Then, too, the pattern of loyalty and disloyalty varies from culture to culture. There is no modern society so satisfying that it does not generate discontent in some of its members. This is inevitable since some individuals need to have grievances and will fabricate them if they do not already exist. In a developing nation, discontent might be generated by economic deprivation and a sense of being unjustly dealt with. In a totalitarian society, it might be created by a pervasive sense of insecurity and a denial of minimal freedom of action. In a wealthy, industrial nation, it might be produced by a feeling of drift and anomie or status apprehension.

In terms of the psychology of motivation, the opposite of the loyal individual may be the person who feels *no* loyalty toward the state, the aloyal or the non-loyal. This aloyal person may be just as capable of disloyal behavior as the one who feels actively hostile toward his country. Usually, however, he remains loyal if he is never severely tested. But, since his attachment to the nation is weak or non-existent, he is prone toward disloyalty once the opportunity presents itself. The G.I. who drifts into disloyal behavior in a Korean prisoner-of-war camp is a far cry from the fellow traveler who deliberately lays plans to defect to the Soviet Union. Both behave disloyally, but, whereas one suffers from aloyalty, the other has substituted a new loyalty for the displaced national loyalty. Whereas one may be apolitical, the other may be totally mobilized politically.

Nevertheless, the concepts of "loyalty" and "disloyalty" tend to be treated as polar opposites. Presumably, they represent clear-cut alternatives and exhaust the behavioral possibilities. It is rather like suggesting that a man has only two emotions, love and hate, and that those persons he does not love he must necessarily hate. At the *behavioral* level, loyalty and disloyalty may be polar opposites, but, in terms of psychology, they must be coupled with aloyalty, and should be seen as points on a continuum.

In any discussion of loyalty and disloyalty, it is important to distinguish the psychology of the individual, on the one hand, from his behavior, on the other. For one thing, the evolution of a man's thought and the evolution of his behavior may follow quite different time schedules. His thinking might evolve over a period of years, and he might be quite incapable of identifying a given moment and saying, "At that moment, my thoughts became disloyal." Furthermore, he might be disenchanted or disloyal in his mind for years before he took an overt action that was disloyal. Just as the loyal individual may, by virtue of circumstances, behave in a way that is termed "disloyal," so the individual who is no longer psychologically loyal may continue to behave in a loyal manner.

It would be mistaken to assume that disloyal behavior is necessarily neurotic or irrational and that the traitor must in some way be mad. He may be, but he need not be. Given the values that an individual holds and the circumstances that surround him, treason may be a thoroughly rational form of behavior. Suppose the duly established government is a tyrannical government. How much should the individual put up with for the sake of loyalty and stability? At what point should he take arms against corruption, inefficiency, and tyranny? If a government is evil, should not the individual do everything in his power to overthrow it—including the acceptance of aid from a foreign power? To be loyal to the government in such circumstances would mean being disloyal to one's deepest beliefs. Under some circumstances, then, treason might be the only rational and appropriate response to tyranny.

To note that the withdrawal of loyalty from a nation may be perfectly rational is not to say that it need be feared, in most cases, on a day-by-day basis. Men do not arise each morning and calculate anew the pros and cons of continued loyalty throughout the day. A society could not function long if its only cement were a continuing calculation of interest. Instead, there are powerful forces at work supporting loyalty to the nation, such as habit, conviction, and the tendency to conform. These forces normally outweigh calculations of interest and cause loyalty to be almost unconditional.

In times of crisis, however, the conditional nature of this loyalty may come to the fore because few loyalties are unconditional. A man may love his wife, but, if she becomes interested in another man, the husband will soon realize that his love was contingent on his wife's behaving according to a certain code. In the same way, love of one's country usually has a contingent element in it, though this element may be tacit and unexamined. The patriot who says, "Right or wrong, my country!" has probably not given the matter serious thought. When his country is *sufficiently* wrong, he will want some basis for withdrawing his loyalty from it. Let the patriot imagine his country under the rule of a dictator, and he will quickly perceive how contingent national loyalty may be. This is, of course, precisely the conflict that patriots in many lands have faced during the past half-century.

If an individual feels markedly out of tune with his culture, if he feels it is not providing him with enough of the good things of life or that the state is not protecting him adequately, the claims of the national community on his loyalty may become attenuated. He may then discover that his loyalty rested on an unspoken bargain, a contractual premise. "I will give the nation my loyalty *if* it gives me enough of the things I want and need. If the nation does not demonstrate that it deserves my loyalty, it shall not have it." If the gospel of individualism is operationally significant in a society, it may speed the erosion of unthinking loyalty by making calculations of individual interest both customary and respectable. The disloyal may simply be those whose demands are above the normal or whose needs are qualitatively different from those of others.

Loyalty to the nation may also be broken down if it comes into direct conflict with powerful non-national loyalties. These loyalties to family, church, community, or the like, may support and strengthen national loyalty, they may be irrelevant to it, or they may weaken it. When one or more of them comes into conflict with loyalty to the nation, the individual will be torn and his behavior will become less predictable. Yet the outcome of the conflict will not automatically favor the nation. Although some German children reported their parents to the police for anti-Nazi behavior, decisions in favor of the family rather than the state must surely have been more common.

> Non-national loyalties thus play a paradoxical role. Their very strength is the strength of national loyalty. They promote and encourage patriotism. But in conflict situations they also compete with national loyalty. Non-national loyalties are simultaneously the bricks out of which democratic national loyalty is built and

the brickbats with which national loyalty may be destroyed.[3]

Considering the fact that disloyalty is a characteristic of the times, it is remarkably difficult to define it. The problem of perspective is a serious one. Observers in the United States, noting the popularity of the Communist party in France and Italy, are inclined to think of those countries as ridden with disloyalty. Yet, in the eyes of the nationals of those countries, the situation is quite different. Communism is simply one of several competing ideologies and movements, and adherence to it is not popularly regarded as being disloyal. Until it is so regarded, the imputation of disloyalty is inappropriate. Time, circumstance, and public opinion, therefore, play a role in defining disloyalty.

During the period between the two world wars, many Frenchmen desired *rapprochement* with Germany and agitated for it. This was perfectly acceptable behavior during the late twenties and early thirties. Later, however, when Hitler came to power and was preparing to move against France, the expression of this sentiment represented defeatism and disloyalty. The behavior and outlook of individual Frenchmen had not changed, but the situation in which they acted had changed. Where was the dividing line? On what date did their loyal activity become disloyal? Behavior that is loyal at one moment may be deemed disloyal a little later. Similarly, behavior that is loyal in one context may be disloyal in another. And behavior that is loyal from one perspective may be disloyal from another.

Furthermore, it cannot be taken for granted that to be loyal is to be "good." Loyalty is good only if it operates in a context that makes it good. To be loyal to an unworthy object is not good. Thus the individual who was disloyal to the Hitler regime may be more praiseworthy than the one who gave unquestioning loyalty and obedience. If loyalty is good or bad depending on the circumstances (and, of course, on the observer's point of view), then the loyal are not always heroes and the disloyal are not always villains.

In the twentieth century, one man's villain is another man's patriot. The traitor may be a coward—or a man of the highest courage; a scoundrel—or a man of the highest integrity. He may be unprincipled—or he may be driven to treason by the highest of motives. Therefore, the traitor is not always wrong, and the loyal individual is not always right. For example, George Washington and a good many of his American contemporaries were disloyal to their king. If the Revolutionary War had been lost rather than won, they might all have graced a traitor's gallows.

The question must always be: Loyalty to whom or what, and under what circumstances? Rarely does the issue pose itself to an individual in the form: Should I be loyal or disloyal? Instead, it is a question of which, among several competing values, best merits his allegiance.

> The most blatant traitor does not look upon himself as such. He regards his acts as an expression of loyalty to, not disloyalty against. Brutus aided in the assassination "Not that I loved Caesar less, but that I loved Rome more." [4]

The German army officers who plotted against Hitler's life put their loyalty to the army, to the nation, to a sense of right, above their sworn loyalty to the head of the German government. Klaus von Stauffenberg said to a colleague: "Look, let's get to the heart of the matter. I am engaged by every available means in the active practice of high treason." [5] When he was executed on the night of July 20, 1944, his dying words were "Long live our Holy Germany." Hero or traitor?

When the Nazi armies invaded Russia, they were greeted as liberators for a time and many members of the Red army surrendered without serious resistance. As a propaganda maneuver, the Nazis organized a large number of these captives into the ill-fated "Russian Army of Liberation" under the direction of General Vlasov. The soldiers in the Vlasov army thought they were going to help overthrow Stalinist tyranny. Patriots or traitors?

Were those Syrians and Iraqi who connived with Nasser for the establishment of the United Arab Republic patriotic leaders of great vision or base betrayers of their nations? Were the Communist Chinese patriots or traitors in accepting Soviet aid in the overthrow of the Nationalists? Are the Chinese on Formosa patriots or traitors when they accept United States assistance with an eye to replacing the *de facto* government of China?

Were Fidel Castro and Che Guevara liberators or traitors when they accepted informal support from private American citizens to help overthrow the dictator Batista? If they are to be termed "traitors" for helping to overturn the established government of their country, what term shall be applied to those Cubans who are now, with United States support, trying to overthrow the government of Fidel Castro?

The problem of perspective also arises in connection with more mundane examples. The officers of a labor union in a given country may want their union to become a stronger, pro-democratic, anti-Communist force. For the same reasons, the United States government, let us say, wants the union to prosper and offers it covert financial support so it can expand its activities and organize a membership drive. Should the assistance be accepted? To take another example, an effective non-Communist newspaper in a Western European country might be having financial and circulation difficulties. If the paper were to fail, its editorial viewpoint would not be adequately expressed by other papers. A covert financial subsidy from the United States would not only allow it to stay in business but enable it to organize a subscription drive and extend its influence. Should the aid be accepted?

The men in the labor union or the managers of the newspaper are eager to continue the fight against Communism but they may have exhausted all other sources of financing. They may feel that to let the union decline or the newspaper go out of business because of scruples about accepting foreign money would be to aid Communism and thus betray their own country. Victory, they might conclude, goes to the daring and the resourceful. If the Communists have little compunction about accepting foreign support, why should they? The long-run aims of the foreign government might not be the same as those of the newspaper or the union, but for the moment they coincide. Besides, the editors and union leaders might ask, who would be using whom? The foreign government would be using the union and the newspaper for its purposes, but they, in turn, would be using the funds of the foreign government for their own purposes. Furthermore, the transfer of funds from the CIA would be secret. It might be timed to coincide with a "fund-raising drive" by the union or newspaper so that sudden affluence would create no undue stir. Since none of the opposition would know for certain where the money came from, what harm could be done?

The union leaders and newspaper owner and editor might well conclude that the importance of their anti-Communist fight justified the use of means that their fellow citizens would characterize as disloyal. Thus, without bribery, without blackmail, without an extensive campaign of persuasion, the United States would have enrolled the services of several important persons and would have acquired two significant instruments of informal access in the target country. If the operation were exposed, the individuals involved would be castigated as "hirelings of a foreign government" and the union and the newspaper would be discredited, if not ruined. Yet the persons committing these disloyal acts would have acted on the basis of thoroughly patriotic motives.

The line of thinking in this example would not be substantially different from that which might have led an American scientist to cooperate with Soviet agents or a Frenchman to cooperate with the Nazis. It is always easier, however, to see how persons in another land might be moved to help one's own country than to see how one's own countrymen could be induced to help a foreign government. Those who betray us are villains, while those who betray the other side are heroes.

> When William H. Martin and Vernon F. Mitchell defected in August, 1960, President Eisenhower chose to voice personally the nation's indignation and said the traitors deserved to be shot. They had fled behind the Iron Curtain with valuable information on the National Security Agency. When Peter Deriabin, an officer of the KGB, defected to the West in 1954, he was kept undercover by the CIA for five years, so vital was the information he brought over. And when he was surfaced he was wreathed in the cliches of the defecting hero: He had "chosen freedom," he had "thumbed his nose at the Communist dictators," and so on. Basically, he had done exactly the same thing as Martin and Mitchell—betrayed his country, left behind a family which would undoubtedly suffer from his action . . . , and brought secret information as the price of admission to the West.[6]

An individual does not inevitably stay loyal to the values of his society simply because he has been brought up in that society, nor does he inevitably stay *disloyal* once he has become so. In the Cold War, men have often defected from one side to the other only to change their minds and decide they were right in the first instance. There is no escape from the complexity of human behavior and the ambivalence of human motivation. The individual caught between competing loyalties is likely to behave in a variable and erratic way, whether the conflict involves politics, professional, family, or romantic considerations. The interests and attitudes an individual shares with the members of an organization will not, in most cases, exhaust the range of his loyalties. Membership in the group may satisfy some of his needs and loyalties, and it may conflict with others. At some point, given changes in his personality, his situation, and the external environment, he may become ambivalent about continued membership or even try to drop out of the group altogether.

The problems of achieving substantive access to a population are related to the interplay of vertical and horizontal ideologies. A vertical ideology, like nationalism, creates cleavages along geographic lines. Such an ideology unifies persons within an area and sets them apart from those in another area. A horizontal ideology, on the other hand, appeals across geographic boundaries and divides men within a nation on the basis of a principle or an interest—"Workers of the world, unite!"

A purely horizontal ideology is rare, of course. Communism is one in that it offers a standing invitation to men to become involved in the movement regardless of their race, place of birth, or social position. Nevertheless, the ideology is firmly anchored in the Soviet Union and is manipulated to serve the interests of the U.S.S.R. Thus it is a horizontal ideology with a national home. Anyone can join the movement—provided he will accept Soviet leadership. This combination of a horizontal ideology with a strong geographic power base can be an effective one.

Conversely, a vertical ideology, such as nationalism, may sometimes have a horizontal appeal. This is most commonly seen in the case of a minority encased in one state but owing allegiance to another. Hitler, for example, had little trouble in using the appeal of German nationalism to arouse the German-speaking minority in the Sudeten areas of Czechoslovakia. The appeal of Zionism is another, if somewhat different, example.

A characteristic of conflict between vertical and horizontal ideologies is that each tends to be highly vulnerable to the other. The present generation has had ample evidence of the ability of the Soviet leadership to persuade men in other lands to surrender their "bourgeois nationalism" and become "internationalists." In a manipulative tour de force, the Soviet Union has had considerable success in identifying itself with nationalism in the emerging areas. To a great extent, nationalism in these areas *is* anti-colonialism (or, at least, was), and the Soviet Union has been able to associate its dislike of the Western powers with the dislike of the same nations by the emerging countries. The nationalist in a developing area who becomes a Communist may sense no conflict at the outset, but the situation is inherently unstable. Communism is a horizontal ideology, to be sure, but, in practice, it is geared to the national interests of the U.S.S.R. It cannot tolerate any other nationalism if that nationalism begins to assume an active form. The Soviet Union, then, uses the Communist ideology to direct the energies of other nations into the service of the Soviet national interest. The interests of the Soviet Union and the developing nations are not identical, however, and, sooner or later, in each country, this must become clear.

It follows, then, that nationalism is the archenemy of Communism. The Soviet leadership tries to use the Communist ideology to override nationalism in the emerging areas only to discover that Communism itself is being persistently undercut by nationalism. The Soviet leadership also tries to use the Communist ideology to override nationalism within the Soviet bloc and here, too, finds nationalism a persistent and troublesome force. If some men can be persuaded to give up nationalism in favor of Communism, others, perhaps more easily, can be persuaded to give up Communism in favor of nationalism. Thus nationalism led Tito's Yugoslavia out of the Soviet bloc, and its continuing influence can be seen in Albania, Eastern Germany, Hungary, Poland, Rumania, and Czechoslovakia. Only the knowledge that Soviet military force will be used ruthlessly to suppress rebellion, as in Eastern Germany in 1953 and in Hungary in 1956, prevents the nationalist ferment in Eastern Europe from becoming more explosive.

For reasons of national interest, Communist China has refused to accept the Soviet manipulation of Marxist-Leninist theory. Mao Tse-tung now offers himself as the only authoritative interpreter of the true faith. The ideology, as defined by the Chinese Communist leadership, is quite as closely identified with Chinese interests as the Soviet version is with Soviet interests. Thus, two powerful nations are competing for access to other populations on the basis of related but distinct versions of a single ideology, each version being a cloak for an aggressive national purpose.

If an ideology is to penetrate a country, it must be adapted to the psychological needs of its potential adherents and perform certain functions with at least a minimum of effectiveness. It must offer a variety of reasons for joining the movement, and these reasons must correspond to the needs of the target population. Individuals in the pool of potential recruits will be attracted to those elements in the ideology and the movement that correspond most closely to their needs. The prejudiced, for example, were drawn to the anti-Semitism in Nazi doctrines. The anti-democratic authoritarians were attracted by the *fuehrerprinzip*, the leadership principle. The bully boys were attracted by the license the movement gave to sadism and violence, while the lost were swept up in the dynamism of the movement. The appeals of Communism are similar in some respects and different in others.[7] The lost are glad to have an ideology that has an answer for everything, and they are drawn by the promise of the movement to absorb and enfold them. An individual in a developing nation may be drawn by the anti-colonial call that Communism sounds. Another will be attracted by the utopian element, the romanticizing of the "toiling masses" and the easy verbiage about freedom, justice, and an end to exploitation. Some will be attracted by the clandestine aspects of the movement, while others may be drawn by the class-conflict doctrine and the way that it legitimizes hatred and violence.

The ideology must also contain a solvent for older loyalties. Before an individual can be brought within the fold, he has to be freed, at least partially, from his attachment to other institutions and doctrines. To further this, the ideology must be designed to increase the sense of individual alienation, and it should explain to potential followers why they have a right to be discontented with the society of which they are a part. It may also seek to undermine loyalties to a particular government, class, or institution, such as the army.

In addition to the solvent, the new ideology must also offer an alternative set of values, evocative symbols, and doctrines. The individual who is discontented and is reaching out for a new loyalty is likely to have a sense of guilt. Therefore, he needs a doctrine of legitimacy to assure him that he is doing the right thing in transferring his allegiance to new ideas, institutions, and leaders. The justifying doctrines do not need to be altogether convincing, of course, to serve their purpose. When men are inclined to do something anyway, they seldom examine critically the doctrines that urge them onward.

Finally, the penetrating nation must devote attention to the organizational aspects of its task. It is not enough to have people socialized into the desired way of thinking. As every good political organizer is aware, group action requires organization, a principle that applies to both legitimate political activities and to deviant political enterprises. The formula for organizing disloyal behavior is socialization *plus* recruitment.

To a considerable extent loyalty is a group phenomenon. One learns loyalty as a member of a group, and he is sustained in that loyalty by continued group membership. When an individual wanders from the group or finds himself in a competing one, his loyalties are likely to be affected. It is with a sure sense of the psychology of disloyalty and resistance that totalitarian regimes seek to control all groups within society and to eradicate those they cannot control. Without a group to serve as a focal point for organizational efforts and the growth of new loyalties, discontent cannot be transformed into resistance. Therefore, a country that is concerned about being penetrated will want to maintain close surveillance over foreign-sponsored groups within its borders, while the penetrating nation, on the other hand, will devote its energies to the establishment of groups.

The process by which a disaffected individual finds his way into a Communist cell is similar in many respects to the way the bohemian finds his way into a comforting Greenwich Village circle. Alienated from the larger society, he is psychologically ready to be absorbed by a deviant group and to let it prescribe his ideas and his behavior and to provide his companions. There are many ways to retaliate at an unfriendly environment besides being disloyal to the nation. In fact, that form of retaliation might not be very satisfying. If the source of the individual's ills lies in immediate personal relationships rather than in the national or international arena, as is usually the case, disloyal behavior may not strike directly at that source.

If, at this critical juncture, however, the individual is drawn into a deviant *political* organization, his discontent may henceforth be given political expression. Suppose, for example, that, instead of becoming a beatnik or joining a religious sect, he becomes involved in the Communist movement. In the first case, his deviation would be politically irrelevant while in the second case he may have started down the path toward active disloyalty. There have been self-recruited traitors, but the loyalty-changing process far more often involves recruiting the individual into a group in which he can build new friendships, develop an altered orientation, learn new attitudes, and fashion new patterns of behavior. Since the alienated individual is likely to be looking for others like himself, his recruitment into such a group may be easy. In a time of international friction and informal access, with nations devoting a great deal of effort trying to influence the people of other countries, a higher percentage of deviant behavior is likely to be channeled into the political realm than would otherwise be the case.

The era of informal penetration is characterized by an increase in the accessibility of populations to ideological appeals from abroad, a development explained partly by the changing technology of communications and partly by the enormous increase in the effort devoted to organization-building as a means of penetration. Men may be socialized into a way of thinking sponsored by a foreign nation without any direct organizational approach, but if radio and printed material are supplemented by personal contact, socialization is likely to be faster, more certain, and more thorough. Once personal contact has been established, political socialization can lead, by easy stages, to political recruitment. After an individual has been recruited, of course, the process of socialization continues and may even accelerate, for the recruit is now provided with companions to serve as models for his own behavior and with a set of group norms and attitudes to reinforce his own. Political socialization and political recruitment, therefore, while analytically separable, are nevertheless likely to be intertwined in practice.

In an earlier period, relatively few organizations were created by one nation as a means of reaching into other nations. Even if widespread disaffection existed in a country, it was difficult, in the absence of organizational machinery, for its enemies to capitalize upon it and turn it into overtly disloyal behavior. The disaffected individual was rarely presented with the operational possibility of disloyal behavior. The situation is now markedly different. From the days of Lenin, Soviet leaders have devoted attention to the strategy and tactics of organizational penetration. Through the years, the Soviet Union has built thousands of organizations in different nations to socialize, recruit, and activate sections of the populace.

The leadership of Communist China, trained in the same school, has also mastered Lenin's lessons. It is not surprising, therefore, that the bitter struggle between the two Communist regimes for influence in the Asian and African nations should be fought, to such a great extent, in organizational terms. In many countries these two powerful actors are contesting to see which will be more successful in building or controlling the organizations into which elite elements are being recruited. In this type of organizational combat, the United States is a weak contender because it is only partly committed to the struggle. Its organizational activities have been limited in scope and primarily defensive. It is simply not in the business of trying to establish organizations in every possible country in order to dominate the politics of the nations concerned. Thus however successful it may be in altering broad public attitudes in a country, it is not equipped to capitalize on those attitudes by recruiting individuals into action organizations.

Americans are often troubled when they read of anti-American demonstrations in a country that is receiving American aid, and in which there is an active information program. The explanation usually lies not in the perversity of the local citizenry or the incompetence of American officials but in the absence of a serious organizational effort. The United States has not trained organizers of various nationalities and it is not trying to build a world-wide network of supporting organizations. When two nations are competing in the informal penetration of a third, the nation that makes the greater organizational effort will have a distinct advantage, other things being equal. Fortunately for the United States, other things are sometimes not equal. The United States may have an advantage of another kind sufficient to off-set the organizational advantage of the Soviet Union or Communist China. It cannot count on having other advantages, however, and Americans should be conscious of the handicap under which their overseas representatives often operate.

In every society, mankind being as it is, there will be individuals whose hold on national loyalty is tenuous and whose grasp of issues is faltering and uncertain. Through most of the history of the nation-state system, these individuals have been safe behind the walls of their nation, shielded from temptation, pressure, and confusion. If their patriotism was lukewarm, it made lit-tle difference. For every man who behaves loyally out of passionate conviction, there are a dozen who conform because of inertia and habit. If an individual of this kind is placed amid a flow of passionate ideological ap-peals, a barrage of claims and counterclaims, charges and countercharges, his behavior becomes problematic. For the first time, he is being tested. The difference be-tween the lukewarm patriot and the active traitor is sometimes one of circumstance. If Eva Toguri had not happened to be in Japan at the time of Pearl Harbor, "Tokyo Rose" might never have been born, and Eva might have gone on to marry one of the young Nisei who were to distinguish themselves during the fighting in Western Europe. If the American soldiers who elected to stay on with the Chinese Communists in Korea had not been captured and tested, they would probably have continued as normal G.I.'s. Neither they nor anyone else would have known that their allegiance to their na-tion and its way of life was shaky.

Informal access makes it possible to test individ-uals on a large scale, and the test may be searching.

Once communication is established with the individual, perhaps via a front group, ideological argumentation seeks to do its work. A line of action is suggested to the individual, perhaps to join a local cell in his city. For the first time, disloyal behavior has become a *practical* possibility. In other words, informal penetration has made disloyal behavior a real option.

Mutually inconsistent ideologies can coexist indefinitely without real conflict if those who subscribe to each one do not come into contact with the other ideology or its adherents. Therefore, until the adherents of one ideology achieve technical access to the adherents of another, the problem of treason and disloyalty is minimal. For example, before the era of informal penetration, there was little technical access. The individual lived in a nation-state that was relatively impermeable. The ideas of the American Revolution could spread eastward to Western Europe, and the ideas of the French Revolution might spread westward to the shores of the United States, but the man in the street could live out his life and never become a proximate target for an ideological appeal from abroad.

On the other hand, introduce into that world a higher level of political and economic interaction, a higher literacy rate, a greater flow of printed communication, a higher level of verbal communication via radio and television. Introduce massive governmental programs designed to reach men and women in other lands by any means possible. Then, gradually, the layers of insulation are stripped away from the individual. Germs of ideas, born aloft by electrical impulses and scattered in all directions, sift downward over the world. All sorts of persons are reached—the strong and the weak, the active and the indifferent, the intelligent and the unintelligent, the informed and the uninformed. The young and impressionable are reached—the discontented, the indifferent, the jealous and vengeful, the cynical, the idealists. Everyone is on the firing line, and no one asks whether this man or that woman is capable of self-defense against ideological attack.

Loyalty is essential to the continuance of a nation, and an attack on that loyalty may amount to a threat to national survival. How great the threat is will depend on the circumstances, and an accurate estimate is often difficult to make. It is easier to underestimate or overestimate the peril than to gauge it accurately. If the danger is underestimated, the security of the nation may be jeopardized. If it is overestimated, on the other hand, internal security measures may become so strict and hysteria so great that individual liberty and freedom of thought and expression may be imperiled.

One characteristic of ideological warfare is that the enemy cannot be readily identified. Neither color, feature, nor language distinguish friend from enemy.

> That is the real horror in the international war of ideologies, that a city does not know whom it houses. The city does not know. The state does not know. Sometimes the individual himself does not know when he ceases to be identified with his own country or from which point of time he became a part of a new movement represented by another country.[8]

No one is happy with this situation, but certain persons find it unnerving and exhilarating at the same time. In every society, there are those who carry anxieties with them wherever they go and who, therefore, must constantly be on the lookout for perils to provide a convincing explanation for the sense of danger and hostility they feel. In a time of tension and informal penetration, these anxious people are more at ease with themselves. There are rumors to circulate, fears to perpetuate, hidden and seemingly innocent enemies to smoke out, public officials to castigate for being "soft" on the enemy or for pursuing a "no win" policy. The superpatriot's almost paranoid sense of impending danger and his genius for finding plots in the most unlikely places guarantee him a leading role in the effort to hunt down and punish the disloyal. Loyalty, of course, will be defined as conformity to the set of prepossessions that the superpatriots currently subscribe to. In making loyalty the supreme value, the superpatriot is unwilling to make concessions to the network of competing values. As always, if any value is made absolute, all other values suffer.

Informal attack provides a non-violent means of attacking a nation-state through the dissolution of the loyalty that binds citizen and nation. It places new demands on the loyalty of the individual, and it means that the leaders of a nation can no longer assume that the citizen will automatically give his primary loyalty to that nation. This chapter has examined the problem of loyalty and disloyalty in the context of one nation's attacking another, and, in that framework, it is easy to assume that the decay of national loyalty is necessarily bad. Whether it is good or bad, however, depends on the circumstances and nature of the competing loyalty. The capacity of the individual to sustain multiple loyalties creates problems, to be sure, but it also makes possible the emergence of new and broader loyalities that include the nation but reach beyond it. It means that loyalty to a regional grouping can develop as well as loyalty to a global institution.

It is comforting that there are positive aspects to the problem of shifting loyalties for that problem is going to remain for the indefinite future. The heightened conflict of loyalties characteristic of the twentieth century is a consequence of the growth of informal penetration. Since informal penetration will remain, and is likely to grow in importance rather than decline, no end to the loyalty problem can be foreseen, although its form may change over the years.

Notes

[1] Margaret Boveri, *Treason in the Twentieth Century* (New York: G. P. Putnam, 1963), p. 7.

[2] Morton Grodzins, *The Loyal and the Disloyal* (Chicago: University of Chicago Press, 1956), p. 5.

[3] *Ibid.*, p. 40.

[4] *Ibid.*, p. 131.

[5] Margaret Boveri, *Treason in the Twentieth Century* (New York: G. P. Putnam, 1963), p. 185.

[6] Sanche de Gramont, *The Secret War* (New York: G. P. Putnam, 1962), pp. 337-338.

[7] Gabriel Almond's *The Appeals of Communism* (Princeton, N. J.: Princeton University Press, 1954) is an excellent study of certain aspects of the psychology of Communism.

[8] Margaret Boveri, *Treason in the Twentieth Century* (New York: G. P. Putnam, 1963), p. 10.

CHAPTER V

International Organizations
and Informal Penetration

Informal access is a general phenomenon in the twentieth century and should not be considered solely in the context of struggle among nations. Nations are vulnerable not only to penetration by other nations but also, in many cases, to penetration by non-governmental organizations and international organizations. The non-governmental organizations providing informal access may be based in one country or may draw their membership from a number of countries. Their number is great and includes such obvious groups as the orders of the Catholic Church, the World Council of Churches, the American Friends Service Committee, the YMCA, the Red Cross, the World Veterans Federation, the Co-operative for American Remittances Abroad (CARE), and the Ford and Rockefeller Foundations. When the history of non-governmental access is written, it will help round out the story of international politics in the twentieth century.

As for international organizations, they are playing an increasingly important part in world politics at both the formal and informal levels. This development has come with remarkable swiftness: the proliferation of leagues, associations, plans, councils, committees, unions, and communities has taken place mostly since the end of World War II. The growth in the number of these organizations is related to the changing nature of the influence that many of them wield. Before the war, the influence of international organizations, such as it was, was felt mainly at the level of external policy. This type of influence, to be sure, is greater now than ever before, but it is no longer the only significant one because international organizations now have a potent influence on the *internal policies* of nations and even conduct significant *operations* within the borders of nations. This increased influence on internal policy is a development of major historical significance. The term "informal penetration," however, will be reserved for those situations in which there are operations by international organizations within a country or direct contact with the people or processes of a country.

The history of informal access by international organizations does not extend far into the past.[1] The International Labor Organization, an affiliate of the League of Nations, marked the first attempt to organize social and economic cooperation on a world-wide scale. It sought to establish liaison with governments, workers' organizations, and employers' associations. The concept of the ILO was limited, however, and it concentrated on research and on the encouragement and coordination of national programs. It did not engage in operational activities any more than did the other technical organizations of the League, such as the Economic and Financial Organization, the Communications and Transit Organization, and the Health Organization. The few emergency operating activities the League was drawn into were on a small scale. Not until the establishment of the United Nations Relief and Rehabilitation Administration in 1943 and the creation of the International Refugee Organization by the United Nations in 1948 did the field operations of international organizations begin to take on real significance.

An inventory of the present operational activities of international organizations would be tedious and quickly dated, since the picture changes from month to month. A few examples may be mentioned, however. The European Coal and Steel Community is a classic example of an organization with a great deal of influence on its members' internal policies. This is, of course, inherent in the notion of a "supranational" organization. The ECSC Treaty enables the organization's High Authority to give a significant degree of direction to two of the major industries in Western Europe, coal and steel. It empowers the community to procure the funds it needs for its activities by means of a levy on the production of coal and steel, a power obviously akin to the power to tax. In addition, the community engages in operations within individual nations, such as providing research grants to industry, grants for the readaptation of workers, and loans for the building of workers' housing. On a day-to-day basis, this supranational organization comes into direct contact with individuals, corporations, and unions in the member countries. Another example is the European Economic Community, whose impact on domestic policy, governmental and nongovernmental, is greater still and is likely to increase if the community reaches more deeply into the field of agriculture.

The North Atlantic Treaty Organization, which can review military planning, defense production, distribution of costs, information policy, infrastructure, and political questions, provides another example of how an international organization can influence the internal policies of members.

The United Nations and its specialized agencies contribute to the changing picture of the operational activities of international organizations. Chapter IX of the United Nations Charter pledges the member states to take joint and separate action for the promotion of "higher standards of living, full employment, and conditions of social and economic development" as well as for "solutions of international economic, social, health and related problems." The Charter pointed in the direction of operational activities, and development along these lines has been rapid.

Several of the specialized agencies connected with the United Nations may be considered briefly here. UNICEF, the United Nations International Children's Emergency Fund, was set up in 1946 on a year-to-year basis and established permanently in 1953. This organization has immunized millions of children against tuberculosis, supplied needy children and nursing mothers with dried skim milk, clothing, and medicines, provided maternal and welfare services, and made available supplies and equipment for milk plants and penicillin factories. A number of other specialized agencies are related to the UN but are not a part of it. The operational activities these agencies conduct are numerous and diverse. The World Health Organization, for example, assists mental health agencies, organizes compaigns for the control of communicable diseases, and trains health administrators, nurses, and laboratory technicians. UNESCO, the United Nations Educational, Scientific and Cultural Organization, disseminates information, arranges for the exchange of persons, and engages in a variety of cultural activities. The Food and Agricultural Organization, the International Telecommunication Union and the International Labor Organization engage in certain operational activities. In addition, specialized agencies such as the Universal Postal Union, the World Meteorological Organization, and the International Civil Aviation Organization possess limited regulatory power. The "Opex" Program, approved by the General Assembly in 1959, involves the sending of officials by the United Nations to newly independent countries to fill the gaps left by departing colonial officials. These individuals are employed by the host country and often have direct and substantial operating responsibilities. Requests for personnel under this program have increased.

The International Monetary Fund, the International

Finance Corporation, and the International Bank for Reconstruction and Development—all specialized agencies of the UN—possess independent financial resources. An agency with funds at its disposal almost inevitably comes to wield influence in the area it is concerned with. When the World Bank, for example, makes a loan to Chile for the improvement of 825,000 acres of pastureland,[2] it has a significant effect on the Chilean economy. Similarly, when its affiliate, the International Development Association, extends credits to Jordan for the expansion and improvement of water supply systems,[3] to Tanganyika for the improvement of the secondary school system,[4] or to Paraguay to improve and increase cattle production,[5] it has an effect upon the internal affairs of those nations. The significance of this development should not be overlooked simply because such influence is now commonplace. It means that a country's internal development is being shaped, not by its own capital-generating processes, nor by private foreign capital seeking profit, nor even by assistance from a foreign government, but by an international organization in accordance with its own purposes. The UN Special Fund and the Expanded Technical Assistance Program, which are parts of the UN machinery but operate largely through the specialized agencies, provide financing and guidance for additional operating activities.

The United Nations Relief and Works Agency for Palestine Refugees in the Near East is an operational organization that carries out relief and works programs in collaboration with host governments. The Intergovernmental Committee for European Migration has aided in the resettlement of one and one-quarter million persons in the last eleven years.[6] At present, it is trying to encourage the settlement of European farmers in Latin America and to improve the reception and placement services there.

The Central American Economic Cooperation Committee, a permanent body of the UN Economic Commission for Latin America, has concluded that the effective functioning of the Central American Common Market (CACM) requires a regional approach to a number of non-economic matters, such as health regulation. This development points in the direction of an increase in operations within the participating nations. The Benelux Economic Union, formally established on February 3, 1958, provides for an intimate relationship among Belgium, the Netherlands, and Luxembourg involving the free movement of goods, persons, capital, and services and extends to the coordination of financial, economic, and social policy.

One of the reasons the picture of informal access by international organizations changes so rapidly is the tendency of organizations without operational activities to acquire them and of organizations having them to expand their scope even further. As new problems are discerned and new needs are agreed upon, it is natural for men to attempt to deal with them within the framework of established organizational machinery. An example of this evolution can be seen in embryonic form with the conclusion of the Executive Board of UNICEF that help for children and young people cannot be regarded as an isolated field of work but must be related to the improvement of conditions in the family, the community, and the nation.[7] The same process may be seen at a somewhat more advanced state of development in the case of the Organization of African Unity. The OAU Charter, signed in Addis Ababa on May 25, 1963, by leaders of twenty-eight African nations, established an organization of limited scope. Yet, at the founding conference, a resolution was introduced and adopted establishing a Commission on Liberation Movements. The principle function of this commission to date has been the collection of funds with which to aid the "freedom fighters" of Angola, Mozambique, and South Africa. The commission has proposed that the member nations make annual contributions for this purpose, which funds it would administer.[8] Thus, almost at birth, this organization moved to establish operations within other nations designed to influence events there.

The relations of the Organization of American States with the Dominican Republic during the years 1960-62 provide an interesting example of the way in which the relatively modest functions formally attributed to an organization by its charter may expand when circumstances are favorable. At the meeting of the OAS foreign ministers at San José, Costa Rica, in August, 1960, the OAS Council was authorized to study the feasibility and desirability of extending existing sanctions against the Trujillo government or of ending them if that regime ceased to be a threat to the peace and security of the hemisphere. The committee created pursuant to this resolution concluded that the Trujillo regime would continue to constitute a danger to peace until certain *domestic* changes were made within the Dominican Republic.[9] This doctrine provided the OAS with a theoretical basis for intervention in the domestic affairs of that country. If a domestic evil generated discontent, the OAS could conclude that such internal discontent was a threat to the peace and, hence, that remedial action was its proper concern. By this two-step argument, the domestic affairs of a nation could be made subject to review by an international organization that lacked formal jurisdiction over the internal affairs of its members.

After giving itself this theoretical justification for intervening in the affairs of the Dominican Republic, the OAS then began to conduct operations of a kind within that country's borders. In October, 1961, the Inter-American Commission on Human Rights visited the Dominican Republic, interviewed a great many persons, and reported to the Balaguer Government (Trujillo having been assassinated) on numerous deprivations of human rights. Furthermore, the "technical assistance" mission sent by the OAS to the Dominican Republic in the fall of 1961 criticized existing arrangements and made extensive suggestions for changes in laws and electoral practices. Finally, a seven-man OAS delegation headed by Secretary-General José Mora observed the December, 1962, elections from a number of points within the country.

The peace-keeping functions of the UN provide a number of examples that show how its functions have expanded and its operational activities have developed. In 1947, the UN Special Committee on Palestine spent some time in that country, and eventually recommended its partition. When this recommendation was accepted by the General Assembly, a UN commission was named to implement it and other recommendations. The UN, therefore, presided over the partition of a disputed area. Then, when the Security Council issued a cease-fire order for Palestine on May 29, 1948, it sent Count Bernadotte and other foreign military observers to supervise its execution. The United Nations, in short, played a critical role in shaping events in Palestine and found it necessary to become operationally involved in the area.

The UN action in Lebanon provides a further example of this expansion of function. The Lebanese had felt threatened by the upsurge of Arab nationalism following the Suez crisis and by the informal penetration activities of Nasser's administration in Egypt. The crisis came to a head in May, 1957. On the 22nd of that month, the Lebanese government requested an urgent meeting of the UN Security Council to hear its charges that the United Arab Republic was endangering international peace and security. The charges, when made, referred to the waging of a press and radio campaign against the government in an effort to incite violence; the supply of arms to rebels; and the infiltration of armed bands from Syria. The U.A.R. spokesman rejected these charges and maintained that President Chamoun's government was seeking to make an international incident of a domestic problem. Nevertheless, as a consequence of the Lebanese charges, a United Nations observation group was sent to Lebanon.

In this case, Country A invited penetration by an international organization to forestall further penetration by Country B. However, Country B argued that the international organization should keep out of A since it had no jurisdiction over domestic matters. If this latter argument had been accepted, the UN would have acknowledged that it had no legal basis for action in cases of informal aggression. The resolution on Essentials of Peace, adopted by the General Assembly in December, 1949, was relevant to the issue since it called upon nations to "refrain from any threats or acts, direct or *indirect,* aimed at impairing the freedom, independence or integrity of any state, or at fomenting civil strife and subverting the will of the people in any state." (Emphasis added.) This extension of the General Assembly's prerogatives opened up a vast range of possible UN actions in the future, including, of course, actions against the United States when it conducts informal aggression.

The UN operation in the Congo also involved a broadening of UN activities. Moreover, it can be used to illustrate several other points relating to UN intervention. Almost immediately after the Republic of the Congo achieved independence on June 30, 1960, rioting and bloodshed broke out. A massacre of Europeans in the Congo threatened, and the government was unable to maintain order. Events began to assume an international cast when Premier Patrice Lumumba asked the United States to send troops to restore order. On July 13, he cabled UN Secretary-General Hammarskjold requesting assistance. On July 14, with Great Britain, France and China abstaining, the Security Council voted to provide assistance in consultation with the government of the Congo. UN military power was thus to be introduced into a country and was to be used for the dual purpose of restoring order and serving as a counterweight to Belgian troops.[10] This objective of restoring order *within* a country was a new one for the UN.

It was hoped, vainly, that the UN force in the Congo (ONUC) could avoid the use of violence. However, military units that are forbidden to use force will seldom find it easy to pacify militant and aroused armed bands. So, before long, ONUC was using force and the size of this UN contingent continued to grow. Just as it was supposed to avoid the use of force, so also it was supposed to avoid political questions and involvement in internal disputes. Yet there was even less chance of fulfilling the second hope than the first. The mere presence of the United Nations force influenced events, and no instructions to the force could alter this. The simple decision to recognize the territorial integrity of the Congo established the frame of reference in which other disputes went forward and was a blow to the secessionist hopes of Katanga leader Moise Tshombe. The decision that UN troops would not be used to crush the rebellion, though the UN disapproved of it, frustrated Lumumba and encouraged him to seek Soviet help. On September 5, President Kasavubu dismissed Prime Minister Lumumba, and the Prime Minister, in turn, dismissed the President. To avoid the extension of civil strife and to prevent the arrival of air-lifted Soviet matériel and advisers, the non-political UN forces closed the airports and shut down the radio stations. UN officials in the Congo repeatedly found themselves in disagreement with the government they had been instructed to collaborate with and at whose invitation they were in the country.

The administrative capacities of the government of the Republic of the Congo had deteriorated badly during the prolonged disputes, and UN technicians, under the direction of Dr. Ralph Bunche, felt compelled to assume steadily broader responsibilities for the administration of the country.

> United Nations technicians are working with nearly all ministries. They are training policemen and soldiers and have taken the country's telecommunications in hand. . . . In such areas as finance, government administration and health services, the United Nations technicians are making surveys of the Congo's needs.[11]

United Nations officials, under instruction to avoid involvement in the internal affairs of the Congo, ended by grappling with virtually all of the interrelated problems associated with the creation of a viable national society there.

Some of the broader lessons of the Congo experience are obvious. A UN action of this kind is inherently interventionist, polite fictions to the contrary notwithstanding. International forces will not find it easy to be non-political when they are thrust into the midst of a bitter power struggle, for any stand they take regarding existing disputes will have political consequences and even the failure to take a stand will have important consequences. In situations that are so acute as to require intervention, it will be difficult to keep this intervention non-violent. If violence has already broken out on a substantial scale, the chances of pacifying the area without resort to violence would normally be slight indeed. It is also clear from the Congo case that the UN presence in a country may not be enough, in itself, to discourage great power intervention. Conceivably, the UN could find itself intervening in a country in competition with a second nation.

The charters of most international organizations proclaim the principle of non-intervention in the domestic affairs of member states. However, when the needs of a situation begin to point toward intervention, the principle of non-intervention is likely to be reinterpreted and a good deal of doctrinal exegesis may be generated as a means of showing what non-intervention "really" means.

The changing complexion of the membership of the United Nations may lead to changes of this kind. The Afro-Asian nations are more keenly attuned to issues of human rights and discrimination than are the Western powers and, perhaps, less alert to issues involving the maintenance of the peace. Since organizations normally adapt to the needs and desires of their members over a period of time or else cease to be effective, the increased voting strength of the Afro-Asian nations may lead, in time, to changes in the United Nations doctrine relating to intervention.[12] The UN may then be able to adopt, within its framework, the doctrine mentioned earlier in connection with the Organization of American States. This would allow the Afro-Asian nations to treat racism within a country as a threat to the peace and therefore as a justifiable basis for intervention. It would thereby rationalize UN intervention in South Africa to end the policy of *apartheid* that is so detested by the Afro-Asian nations.

The rapid growth in the operational activities of international organizations and the extent of the influence these organizations have upon the internal affairs of nations have been little remarked or examined. The lack of attention may be explained by the fact that men have trouble perceiving those things that are contrary to their expectations and preferences. Because, in the past, the influence of international organizations had been largely confined to the external policies of nations, influence on domestic policy was not expected. Furthermore, these organizations were not supposed to exercise that kind of influence because it was not regarded as legitimate. The *practice* of intervention by international organizations in the domestic affairs of nations developed rapidly in response to powerful needs and pressures while the *theory* concerning the proper behavior of such organizations remained wedded to the doctrine of non-intervention.

When institutions do not behave the way they are expected to, men may ultimately have to change their ideas. In the short run, however, a typical human response is the development of fictions that serve to obscure the contradiction between expectation and reality. Thus, for example, all peace-keeping interventions are proclaimed as "non-political" and all assistance activities, no matter how far-ranging and politically significant, are described as "technical." The parallel to the experience of the United States, as outlined in Chapter III, is a close one. In an analogous situation, the United States, albeit hesitantly and tardily, and without fully acknowledging what it was doing, began to develop an ideology that treated intervention as potentially good.

In much the same way, advocates of action by international organizations need to evolve a parallel ideology. They need to develop an ethic of intervention, or an ethic of assistance. The component elements for such an ethic are at hand and are persuasive. Furthermore, it is far easier to develop a convincing ethic of intervention for an international organization than for a nation. After all, a nation is expected to pursue its national interest—narrowly defined—and therefore the idea of disinterested national behavior appears as almost a contradiction in terms. However, few are concerned that UNICEF, let us say, may pursue a UNICEF-interest, or that the World Health Organization may pursue a WHO-interest. An international organization is not automatically assumed to be self-serving, and few persons have difficulty conceiving that its actions may reflect disinterested or generous motivations.

If international organizations are to develop an ethic of intervention, then host nations must develop a complementary set of attitudes. They must come to understand that international organizations can rarely aid the people of a nation that seeks its aid without penetrating it. Therefore, a nation should not seek assistance and, at the same time, try to apply the criteria of non-intervention and non-political activity to the assisting organization.

An ethic of intervention for international organizations must discriminate among organizations and purposes and, hence, must contain conditional elements. Just as intervention by individual nations may be good or bad depending on circumstances, so, too, intervention by international organizations may be good or bad. Intervention is not always bad when a *nation* is intervening and not always good when an international organization is intervening. International organizations have been (and will be) created for the most diverse reasons, not all beneficent, and their behavior will be as diverse as the purposes that brought them into existence.

The behavior of even well-established organizations may be indeterminate at times, for an international organization does not have a mind or soul to guide it along a consistent path. There is no General Will determining the actions of the United Nations, for instance. Calling an organization "international" does nothing to remove its decision-making processes from the political arena. Its decisions will still be produced by a political process, one that reflects the preferences and relative strengths of the nations involved. Each nation concerned with a decision will attempt to shape that decision according to its own wants, needs, and policy preferences, supporting intervention in one case and opposing it in the next, restricting its scope in one case and seeking to expand it in another.

Since the process is political and reflects the varying strengths of the contestants, the ability of nations to influence the final decision of an international organization will normally vary greatly. If a nation is powerful in the councils of an organization, it may be able to direct the action of that organization along the lines it tavors. As a case in point, the role of the United States in the United Nations during the early years of that organization's existence was an exceptionally powerful one, and its influence was felt on matters both great and small.

Certainly, in the absence of a United States decision to resist the invasion of South Korea by North Korean forces in June, 1950, it is hard to see how the UN could have taken effective action against that breach of the peace. When an international organization is relatively inactive, it is sometimes possible to minimize the role of the great powers in it. On the other hand, when the challenge that it faces requires the large-scale mobilization of skills, resources, and power, the position of the great powers within it is automatically magnified. Therefore, the influence of the United States on the UN decision to resist aggression in Korea was very great, and, after the decision, the UN forces in Korea were placed under the direction of American military leaders. It is noteworthy that the United States government was not eager to have the organization supervise the military and political actions it took in Korea in the UN's name; a proposal by the Secretary-General to establish a "Committee on Coordination of Assistance to Korea," composed of six members of the Security Council with the Secretary-General acting as *rapporteur,* was rejected by the United States. To sum up, then, an international organization may intervene in a nation either because its decision-making process is dominated by one or a few nations or because of a genuine consensus among its members. Whatever the basis of the decision, the fact remains that the tempo of intervention has increased in recent years.

As the significance of international organizations in world politics expands, the way that decisions are made in these organizations must automatically become a more pressing question. If international organizations are developing into mighty engines for social change, who is to guide them? How is the decision made that commits the UN to this informal action and prevents it from taking that formal action?

Notes

1 Walter R. Sharp, *Field Administration in the United Nations System* (London: Stevens and Sons, Ltd.; New York: Frederick A. Praeger, 1962), p. 13ff.

2 IBRD Press Release 63/52, December 19, 1963.

3 IDA Press Release 63/14, December 12, 1963.

4 IDA Press Release 63/15, December 20, 1963.

5 IDA Press Release 63/16, December 26, 1963.

6 "International Organizations: Summary of Activities," in *International Organization,* XVIII, Number 3, Summer, 1964, p. 669

7 UNICEF Document E/ICEF/448.

8 "The Organization of African Unity," Norman J. Padelford, *International Organization,* XVIII, Number 3, Summer, 1964, p. 537.

9 See the interesting discussion by Jerome Slater, "The United States, the Organization of American States, and the Dominican Republic, 1961-1963," *International Organization,* XVIII, Number 2, Spring, 1964, p. 276. "Thus, under this formula, the door had been opened for the OAS to involve itself in what had hitherto been considered the purely internal affairs of its member states."

10 See "UN Forces and Lessons of Suez and Congo: An Appraisal," Herbert Nicholas, in *International Military Forces,* Lincoln P. Bloomfield, editor (Boston: Little, Brown, 1964), pp. 102-127.

11 *The New York Times,* July 26, 1960.

12 See Ali A. Mazrui, "The United Nations and Some African Political Attitudes," *International Organization,* XVIII, Number 3, Summer, 1964.

CHAPTER VI

Informal Penetration

and the Nation-State System

The advent of informal penetration on a large scale adds an important new dimension to international politics. When a potent new factor is introduced into a system of interrelated parts, every part of that system will be affected to a greater or lesser extent, as will be the relationships among the parts. In Chapter IV, for example, the impact of informal penetration on individual loyalty was examined. This chapter will note the impact of informal penetration on:

(1) the nature of power in world politics;
(2) patterns of conflict and competition among nations;
(3) international stability;
(4) the role of international organizations on the world scene;
(5) the nature and functioning of the nation-state;
(6) the nature and functioning of the nation-state system.

The implications of informal penetration for the exercise (and analysis) of power in the international realm are intriguing, if shrouded in uncertainty. The capacity of a nation to conduct an informal attack is by no means the same thing as its capacity to wage a military campaign, yet it may be quite as important. To a degree, a nation's ability to wage total or limited war, on the one hand, and to engage in informal attack, on the other, are independent variables. The fact that these two capacities can vary independently creates several logical possibilities.

For one thing, a nation may be powerful in traditional terms and also have a substantial capacity for informal aggression. The Soviet Union is an example at the present time. Another possibility is a nation that is strong in traditional terms and weak in its capacity for informal aggression. Some years ago the United States would have provided an example of this combination. Or, a nation might be weak in both respects.

More interestingly, however, a nation might be weak in traditional terms and yet strong in the area of informal aggression. One that is relatively poor with regard to resources, population, and military power may yet possess notable capabilities for informal attack. Do such nations exist?

Nasser's Egypt is an example. It is weak according to the traditional indices of power and was even weaker during the early years of Nasser's regime. Nevertheless, by means of agitation, political threats, terrorism, the propaganda of Radio Cairo, the appeal of pan-Arabism, and the conception of a United Arab Republic, this weak country has had a marked effect on the political climate of the entire Middle East. In a period of six months in 1963, Yemen, Iraq, and Syria all experienced coups by groups favorably disposed toward Nasser and the United Arab Republic. Cuba presents a second example. Fidel Castro, in the period immediately after coming to power—and with few of the traditional resources at his command—managed to throw a sizable portion of Latin America into turmoil with his efforts to foment revolution in neighboring countries. There is no inherent reason, therefore, why informal aggression, including attempts at *coups d'état,* cannot be designed and promoted in Cairo, in Havana, or in the capitals of other small countries quite as well as in Moscow or Washington or Peking.

Informal penetration alters the way in which the nations of the world compete with one another. This is true of both the lesser powers and the great powers. Figure 6.1 suggests some of these competitive relationships in a bipolar world. Nations 1, 2, 3, and 4 are within the ambit of Nation A. Nations 5, 6, 7, and 8 are within the ambit of Nation C. The remaining ones, 9 through 14, are in neither one camp nor the other, although they are not necessarily all equidistant from the two poles. This last group would be neutralist, or non-aligned.

Nation A will normally have great access to the nations within its immediate zone of influence, less access to the non-aligned nations, and still less to those under the sway of C. But it will try to draw Nations 5, 6, 7, and 8 out of C's zone of influence and into the area of the non-aligned, and it will probably try to draw the non-aligned closer to its own position.

If Nation A alone were trying to penetrate one of the non-aligned nations, for example, Nation 12, it would

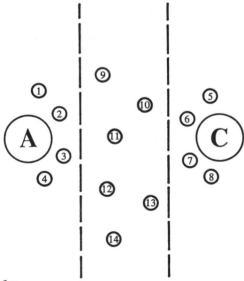

Figure 6.1

have a monopoly position. If A were using attack techniques, 12 would be alone in countering them. Or, if A were relying on support techniques, it could insist that 12 grant substantial concessions in return for its support. But, once C enters the competition, A's monopoly would be destroyed. Indeed, monopoly might be replaced by monopsony, that is, a situation in which the buyer rather than the seller sets the price at which they will deal. More than once, countries have threatened to accept aid from the Soviet Union if the United States did not satisfy this or that demand. For a time, for example, the United States and the Soviet Union contested for the privilege of financing the Aswan High Dam for Nasser's Egypt. Because of the powerful bargaining position of the recipient nation in a competitive situation, a program that starts out as one of attack may end up as a program of support.

Before C makes a serious effort to penetrate Nation 12 in competition with A, it should assess its prospects. If the target is heavily dependent on A, then C will find it difficult to make appreciable progress. A developing country that falls within the sphere of influence of a major country will normally be highly vulnerable to penetration by that country. In addition to governmental access, there may be a good deal of non-governmental and quasi-governmental access. This disproportionate dependence on one of the major powers may be due to geographic position, economic ties, or historical background. The relation of the Latin American countries to the United States may be cited as an example.

When two nations attempt penetration of a third, each may have limited initial success without serious conflict, provided neither aims at the same organizational targets as the other. If the two movements are aggressive, however, conflict is inevitable since both will be trying to achieve influence in, or recruit followers from, the same pool of potential supporters. Beyond a certain point, the success of one penetrating nation will mean the failure of the other if the target nation is not large enough to sustain the growth rate that each of the penetrating powers insists upon.

Informal access is an important feature of a bipolar power pattern and of any contemporary power configuration. Figure 6.2 depicts schematically a three-way competition for access and influence among the United States, the Soviet Union, and Communist China. Just as the United States and the Soviet Union are competitively seeking to penetrate certain countries, in the same way, the Soviet Union and China are competing for access to countries such as Albania, Yugoslavia, Poland, and nations in Southeast Asia and Africa. In addition, the United States and China are competing vigorously for influence in nations such as South Vietnam, Cambodia, and Pakistan.

There are a number of reasons for concern about the impact of informal penetration on the stability of the international system. For one thing, the techniques of informal attack can be highly effective under favorable conditions. The covert subsidy of one or two newspapers in a country could make a substantial difference in the complexion of public thought. The injection of a modest sum into its labor movement at the right time and place could significantly alter the direction of a country's development. Organizing a guerilla movement can create grave difficulties for a government or even lead to its overthrow. In Malaya, for example, a guerilla movement supported from the outside achieved its minimum objective of harassing the British; in Indo-China a guerilla movement (converted in the final stages of the conflict into a regular army) achieved its maximum objective of driving the French out of the area. The organization of a successful *coup d'état* can change the entire political orientation of a nation.

Informal attack can sometimes achieve substantial results and it is an economical mode of attack at the same time. This type of attack often depends upon the vigor,

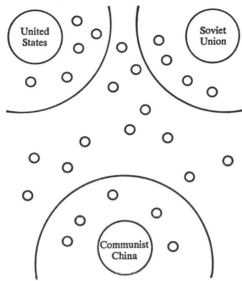

Figure 6.2

skill, and inventiveness of a relatively small number of persons. A nation engaging in it will seek to exploit the energies of others, but it need not deploy vast armies of its own citizens. Funds and material are needed, to be sure, but the expenditure is of a different order of magnitude from that needed to develop modern military power. Therefore, it allows a nation to think of millions rather than billions. Political turmoil can sometimes be created in a given country by the expenditure of a few million dollars, and governments of small countries have been overturned for little more. Guerilla movements offer another example. They are relatively inexpensive to organize and operate; yet it is costly and difficult to suppress them, as the painful experience of the United States in South Vietnam illustrates.

Aggressively inclined nations that would be foreclosed from playing a major role in international affairs by the cost of modern weaponry will find that informal aggression has much to recommend it. Traditionally, a nation's imperial ambitions have been sharply limited by its resources and general power position. In the realm of informal attack, however, resources go a long way. If a small nation chooses to concentrate its efforts (or if it has access to outside support), it can become quite influential in a restricted area. That is to say, a nation may now be imperialist on a shoestring. This is a development that various nations will not be slow to appreciate.[1]

The time required for developing an informal attack capacity is modest. By contrast, there is a limit to the rate at which a nation's overall strength can be increased, since it involves such factors as the level of education and training of the population, the availability of resources, and the level of development of the economy. But, with relatively little time and effort, a nation with a small informal attack capacity can expand its capabilities four- or fivefold. For example, after coming to power, neither Nasser nor Castro lost much time in developing the informal attack capacities of their nations.

Another advantage is that informal attack permits an aggressively inclined nation to probe for weak spots without forcing it to take overtly aggressive action. It need not deliver an ultimatum to its neighbor, or declare war, or invade. Instead, it can attack that neighbor informally while maintaining correct relations formally. And the nation attacked may be left without grounds for a formal protest. Indeed, it may be some time before it realizes that it is under attack.

A nation undertaking covert indirect attack usually takes some pains not to become formally involved. This allows it to disengage from the undertaking, if this course seems advisable, with a minimum loss of prestige. If a project does not develop favorably, it is quietly liquidated or allowed to taper off while attention is centered elsewhere.

A nation will try not to have its covert activities exposed, but, if they are exposed, the penalty is not always great. There is a period of embarrassment to be sure, but it may be soon forgotten. After it becomes widely known that a nation is engaged in this activity, and after it has been caught in the act several times, each new discovery occasions progressively less shock and surprise. The Soviet Union, for example, is beyond any reaction other than a momentary embarrassment. But, a nation like the United States that attaches a good deal of importance to its moral position will suffer relatively more from exposure. That is why the U-2 incident and the abortive Cuban invasion both seemed grievous blows at the time.

Traditionally, the defeat of a nation in its policies of aggrandizement has been costly. Military defeat can alter the history of a nation or even lead to its liquidation. Defeat in an informal attack, however, although it may vary from the disappointing to the serious, is rarely catastrophic. Hence, defeat in such projects may be borne with a degree of equanimity.

An appreciation of the possibilities of informal attack may have an effect on the policies a nation will pursue. An objective that was outside the bounds of possibility as long as that nation confined itself to orthodox thinking might appear very different if that nation stretched its horizons to include informal attack. Thus, a change in technique can lead to a change in objectives, while a change in objectives opens up new opportunities for the use of a technique. The two thus go hand in hand.

The number of nations engaging in informal penetration is likely to increase. The factors that make informal attack attractive to the great powers will have even stronger appeal to the smaller nations.

Not only is the number of nations engaging in informal attack likely to increase, but the number of operations carried on by each nation may also increase. It is a truism of foreign policy that a nation should husband its resources and not overcommit itself. But the real question is what constitutes *"over*commitment" during an era of informal penetration. In terms of alliances, solemn guarantees, and the deployment of military forces about the globe, there is a real possibility of overcommitment. Informal attack is different, however. Characteristically, a nation using this approach makes no formal commitments, can disengage itself with little loss of prestige, can expand its Cold War capabilities rapidly, and can engage in these activities on a moderate budget. A nation of modest resources might, therefore, conduct three, four, or a half-dozen informal operations simultaneously. This means that the question of "overcommitment" of a nation's power is markedly altered and eased when the matter is considered from the standpoint of informal aggression.

Instability in the international system is promoted by the emergence of new states that make excellent targets for attack and by the existence of three major power centers willing and able to encourage and finance the informal attack activities of a variety of nations. In addition, nations not aggressively inclined may, when they find themselves under informal attack, be forced to respond in kind.

The general level of accessibility in the international system has increased in recent decades. However, it is not evenly distributed. Some nations are highly vulnerable; others are far less so. Conversely, some have virtually no access to populations outside their borders, while others have a great deal. This uneven distribution of attack and defense capabilities promotes instability in international relations. When a great power, such as the Soviet Union, combines a low level of internal penetrability with a high level of access to other nations, its behavior can seriously affect the stability of the international system.

All of the factors mentioned above will encourage nations to probe for weak spots in the defenses of their neighbors. If a given project works, well and good. If it does not, little has been lost in the way of prestige, personnel, or material. When victories of any degree can be achieved in the realm of informal attack, they are likely to be excellent investments, providing a large yield in return for a modest risk. Such a situation is one that encourages adventurism in nations both great and small.[2]

The considerations mentioned above create a somber picture. The *attack* potential of informal access is great and has an undeniably unsettling effect on international stability. It should not be overlooked, however, that informal *support* measures provide their users with means for increasing stability. The access of the United States government to the nations of Western Europe after World War II, for example, took many forms, including that of economic aid. Access, in this case, was used to promote stability. United States support for the European integration movement, expressed through a variety of formal and informal means, was also a factor promoting long-range stability. Furthermore, the access of the United States government to Latin American nations is being used to promote changes designed to increase stability in Latin America.

International organizations can be a source of stability or instability in world politics, depending upon the purposes they are invested with and the wisdom with which they are used. The United Nations, for example, contributes to international stability in a number of important ways. The very existence of that organization, and the degree of success it enjoys in mobilizing opinion on some issues, has undoubtedly helped deter nations from mischievous behavior. Then, too, the peace-keeping actions it has undertaken, and the knowledge that these powers may be exercised again, have probably had a stabilizing effect as well.

The operational activities of the United Nations and of various other international organizations also have an important impact on international stability. The short-run effects may be settling or unsettling, but, in the long run, these activities will, in all likelihood, tend to increase international stability. It is hard to imagine a satisfactory level of stability in a world in which there are gross disparities in living styles about which nothing is being done. To the extent that the nations of the world, through the United Nations, are beginning to posit a common international responsibility for tackling the problem and are beginning to take action on it, they are probably having a stabilizing effect.

Since informal attack is a critically important form of conflict in the contemporary world, it is worth asking whether stability may be increased by some form of disarmament in this realm. Other than within the context of a general reduction in the level of international tension, however, the prospects for disarmament do not appear good. For one thing, an attacking nation is likely to find it hard to negotiate about covert activities that it denies having any connection with. Furthermore, it would be exceedingly hard to police a disarmament agreement dealing with informal attack since many attack operations are covert. By way of contrast, an army, once created, cannot be hidden; airfields and missile launching facilities can probably be detected by one means or another. Covert informal attack, on the other hand, can be so shrouded in secrecy, or so confused by claims and counterclaims, that the truth is hard to come by. It is one thing for a UN peace observation commission to police a border in order to determine whether arms and men are crossing it and quite another thing to try to learn the "facts" about subversion or to guard against political penetration.

The full implications of informal penetration for international stability will probably not be clear for some time to come. The attack potential was developed somewhat earlier than the support potential and it has also received a heavy share of the headlines because of the world's preoccupation with the Cold War. As the support activities of individual nations and international organizations develop over the years, assuming no catastrophe, something closer to a balance between the stabilizing and destabilizing forces of informal penetration may be struck. A good deal will depend on whether informal attack activities or informal support activities have the greater capacity for growth and elaboration. On the whole, however, the long-term picture does not encourage optimism.

In the preceding chapter, it was suggested that the contemporary role of international organizations might be better grasped if an "ethic of intervention" or an "ethic of assistance" were developed to explain this behavior. International organizations provide a means by which a number of the most vexing problems in world affairs may be tackled. In some instances, an international organization may be simply *one* of the ways that an attack on a problem may be made, in another instance it may be the *best* way, and in others it may be the *only* way.

International organizations are also becoming a progressively more important means for diffusing knowledge, skills, and resources throughout the world. This diffusion process, aided, of course, by the programs of individual nations, is without historical precedent. It will have a profound effect on the development of the emerging nations and on the processes of social change throughout the world. Within a decade, allowing for acceleration, institutionalized cultural diffusion will be one of the most powerful formative influences at work in the world. In addition, as already noted, international organizations can play an important role in promoting international stability through their peace-keeping activities.

Viewed in this light, the rationale for intervention by international organizations is a powerful one. It explains (and justifies) the increasing influence they are having on the domestic policy decisions of nations and the developing web of operational activities that often reaches deep into the internal life of nations.

As for the nation-state, informal penetration changes its functioning in a number of vital respects. One of the state's primary functions has been to define territorial boundaries and to control movement across them. To-day, however, most states are either unwilling or unable to control fully the movement of funds, persons, ideas, information, and material across their borders. To speak of the informal access that many nations now have to one another is to say that territorial boundaries do not have the meaning they formerly had. It follows, then, that traditional lines between nations are becoming blurred. The Eastern European satellite nations provide one example and the developing European Community provides another. In a period of increasing informal access, a situation sometimes develops in which the critical boundary may not be the geographic one but one defined by the circumstances of the market, the location of the adherents of an opposing ideology, the location of a given race or religious group, or the zone of effectiveness of counterpenetration efforts.

Another important function of the state is to defend its citizenry and repel attack. While this has not always been easy, or even possible, the nature of the task has usually been clear-cut, and the country under attack rarely had any doubt about the matter. The advent of informal access to nations, however, has introduced new and subtle forms of aggression. Conflict becomes far more varied. Aggression is harder to identify and deal with. Instead of an ultimatum, there may be the quiet infiltration of labor organizations and the preparation of a series of carefully organized "spontaneous" riots and strikes. Instead of a declaration of war, there may be the formation of a militant Communist party and the systematic infiltration of student, youth, veterans', and cultural organizations. And, instead of an armed thrust across a border, an "attack" may take the form of the establishment of a government-in-exile and the organization of anti-government resistance forces. The first indication a government may have that it is in serious difficulty is when a foreign-sponsored *coup d'état* erupts. In short, the obligation of a state to defend its citizenry and territory has changed, and its task has been made a good deal more difficult by the development of the techniques of informal attack.

The state traditionally has had a monopoly of armed forces within its borders. If that state is under informal attack, however, guerilla units or the combat adjuncts of a militant party may also wield substantial power. These paramilitary formations destroy the force monopoly of the government, whether they are used against the government itself or against other parties and organizations.

Historically, the rulers of one society have often challenged the claim to legitimacy of the rulers of another society, and these disputes have generally proceeded within the framework of an agreed principle of legitimacy, such as monarchy based on hereditary succession. In an era of informal penetration, however, the attack on the legitimacy of the government in the target country frequently denies the very principle of legitimacy on which that government is based or reinterprets it in a significantly different way. In a colonial area, the legitimacy of colonial rule will be denied. Dictatorial governments or governments based on a military junta will be denounced on the grounds that only rule based on the free consent of the governed is legitimate. If a country has democratic institutions, they may be undercut by the argument that the state is the instrument of the dominant class and that bourgeois democracy is not democracy at all.

One of the traditional functions of the state has been to promote symbols and ideals designed to create loyalty to the nation and unity within it. Thus the state teaches that loyalty to the nation is a value of supreme importance, and most citizens respond with the complementary attitude that disloyalty is abominable. In the present period, however, a nation having access to another may offer alternative symbols in an effort to create division and to break down loyalty. While the government of the target country is trying to reduce conflicts within the populace, agents of the penetrating nation may be working hard to exacerbate them. And, while the government is teaching loyalty, the penetrating power is busily trying to persuade the people that values such as justice, the proletariat, socialism, fascism, or democracy take precedence over nationalism. Treason is thus presented as a higher loyalty. In other words, loyalty to the nation is challenged by a transnational appeal that seeks to reach out across national boundaries. The effectiveness of this type of appeal has been demonstrated repeatedly during recent decades. Thus, it can no longer be assumed that men will automatically give their primary loyalty to their own nation. It would be hard, therefore, to find a more direct attack on nationhood than the undermining of the loyalty, the spirit of nationalism, that supports the nation.

Characteristically, the nation-state has been a self-contained decisional unit. It might be subjected to severe external pressure, but its decision as to how it would respond to that pressure and what course it would pursue in its domestic affairs remained its own. Rarely did agents of one nation participate in an intimate and continuing way in the domestic affairs of another. Now, however, this participation is an everyday occurrence. The United States, for example, has many thousands of employees abroad who are urging other nations to introduce this or that agricultural technique and helping them to do it, who are building roads, helping to organize social reform, seeking greater voting honesty, initiating programs of health and sanitation, instructing in the arts of administration, setting up new banking systems, organizing land reform, training officers and men in the military services, establishing schools, guiding fiscal and monetary policy, reforming the tax laws, and so on.

The Soviet Union directs Communist parties and organizations in scores of countries. Through this means and a variety of others, it seeks, and often achieves, an influence over the decision-making of nation-states. Countries that were once left to solve their problems by their own devices now find that these problems are of absorbing interest to outsiders who cheer, groan, agitate, and intervene in what, only a short time ago, would have been regarded as matters of purely domestic concern. No longer can it be automatically assumed that a country is a self-contained decisional unit simply because it is included, with other countries, in the category of "nation-state." One nation may now exert external pressure upon another and, going far beyond that, may reach inside the target nation and influence its decision-making processes. Thus, a government may be interested not only in shaping policy and opinion within its own borders but in other countries as well.

An important part of the explanation for the decline of the nation-state as a self-contained decisional unit is to be found in the widespread need for assistance felt by so many nations during the years since the end of World War II. The European nations responded to Secretary of State George Marshall's initiative by requesting large-scale aid from the United States. The urgency of their needs more than offset their hesitation about informal American influence. Now, for the newer nations of the world, economic development is a primary objective. They have learned, however, that they cannot achieve that goal unaided. Proud of their new-won political independence, these nations are finding that pressing needs quickly lead them into embracing economic dependency. They have sought help from the developed nations and, as they have grown in number and political influence, have pressed international organizations for more and more assistance—capital resources, supplies, equipment, training facilities, advisory services, and demonstration projects.

At each step of the way, the concrete advantages to be gained from such assistance have outweighed the shadowy disadvantage involved in surrendering such an intangible as territorial inviolability. As a result, informal penetration has removed much of the substance behind the concept of sovereignty. Except in a formal or legal sense, this concept has little application or use in a world in which nations continually interact and interpenetrate and in which there are international organizations such as the United Nations, broad alliances such as NATO, and supranational organizations such as the European Economic Community.

Six factors associated with the informal access of nations to one another have been mentioned, and each of them undermines an important aspect of nationhood. Taken together, they suggest the quiet and gradual disappearance, not of the nation-state to be sure, but of the *inviolable* nation-state. Since nation-states are the building blocks of the international system, anything that modifies their nature and functioning in a significant way must necessarily have a powerful effect on the functioning of the nation-state system as a whole.

In attempting to assess the overall significance of informal penetration for the nation-state system, it should be noted that the growth of the influence of international organizations, the growth of their operational activities, and the growth of informal penetration by individual nations have all taken place during the same time span. This is not accidental, for they are simply different, linked aspects of a single process—the progressive breakdown of the inviolable nation-state. The increase of informal penetration by nations and by international organizations results from changes in the nation-state system and, at the same time, stimulates further changes in that system. As the borders of individual states became porous, international organizations and other nations moved in to take advantage of that porosity. By the same token, their moving in created the conditions that the next wave of nations and organizations was able to exploit. Informal penetration, therefore, is both the result of a breakdown of national borders and a cause of the breakdown.

As the inviolable nation-state became, for the most part, a thing of the past, vast new areas were opened up for exploitation by international organizations. The last two decades, consequently, have been full of innovation in the field of international organization. A rich crop of new organizations and techniques for dealing with regional, functional, and world-wide problems has been developed. The United Nations, with its Secretariat, its array of special agencies, investigative commissions, supervisory commissions, and assistance missions, is only the most spectacular example.

International organizations have thus become increasingly important actors on the international scene, and the trend toward increasing specialization, complexity, and breadth of coverage may be expected· to continue. Once the decision-makers of a nation become primarily concerned with identifying and solving problems—of labor, health, child welfare, agriculture, industrialization, trade—questions of national prestige and sovereignty are automatically given a back seat. This change, when it takes place, represents a significant breakthrough in the development of international organization. When men cease to be preoccupied with questions of geographical jurisdiction, they are freed to attack a range of problems on the basis of need, convenience, and functional organization.

To be sure, some nations have managed, with a degree of success, to conduct their operations with other states through the channels provided by international organizations. They have been able to do this when the decision-making apparatus of the organization is so structured that it reflects the preponderant position of one or a few members. The entry of an international organization into an operational field characterized by informal access, therefore, is sometimes the consequence of consensus among its members concerning the organization's mission and sometimes a scarcely-veiled form of informal penetration by influential nations. But neither of these bases for the activity of international organizations should be emphasized at the expense of the other.

The formal and legal powers of a nation-state remain the same when a nation is penetrated by other nations or an international organization, but the underlying reality is likely to be profoundly changed. With relatively few exceptions, such as the small-scale activities of missionaries and educators, the historical pattern has been one of a virtual monopoly of operations within a country by the government and people of that country. Now, often sanctioned by the government of a country, outside agencies are performing a variety of functions within its borders.

For a good many years, analysts of international politics have argued that the nation-state system was obsolete because technology was shrinking the globe, because the war-making power of the larger states made national sovereignty irrelevant, because of economic interaction, and because nationalism appeared to stand in the way of a stable organization of the peace. This has been a depressing line of thought since it was quite apparent that nation-states were not going to destroy themselves by their own hands.

During the period in which these attitudes were becoming widespread, however, the new wine of informal access was being poured into the old bottle of the nation-state system. The development of informal access modified the very feature of the system that observers found most abhorrent, that is, territorial inviolability. This progressive adaptation of the nation-state system has not taken place in response to a conscious effort to make the multistate system workable. The revolution has, in fact, taken place virtually without being noticed. This does not mean that the system changed autonomously. Instead, individual decision-makers, in trying to cope with an array of pressing and immediate problems, made thousands of decisions that had the cumulative effect of modifying the structure of the nation-state system as a whole.

The revolution may not go far enough fast enough, but, if the multistate system does prove viable and adaptable over the next few generations, the explanation may lie in the development of informal penetration. Informal access replaces inviolability with interpenetration and, in so doing, markedly improves the survival possibilities of the nation-state system—and of mankind.

The increase in the fluidity of national frontiers is a change of first importance, and its consequences will spread in many directions for many years. But, like most great changes, it is two-faced: it opens up possibilities for both good and evil. It produces new forms of attack—and the institutions and techniques that may be able to cope with these attacks. It allows men to commit aggression against their fellow men in clever new ways —and promotes the use of new modes of collaboration. It ushers in a Cold War—and promotes generosity and international helpfulness on an unprecedented scale. It makes it easier to use ideology as an instrument of aggression—and makes it harder to maintain an Iron Curtain or a Bamboo Curtain that will protect an ideology from contamination and challenge. It undermines established loyalties—and makes it possible for new, broader loyalties to emerge and to pass across national boundaries. It provides new means for generating political instability—and allows the development of techniques and institutions to achieve stability. It undermines the nation-state system—and helps make it viable and adequate to the needs of the time.

Because the advent of informal access creates both problems and possibilities, it may not be clear for some time whether the net result is to improve or worsen the world situation. Informal access promotes the flow of communication, but it does not guarantee increased understanding. Beneficent transnational loyalties may or may not develop. Men may or may not learn the habits of cooperation by working together to meet common needs—or, they may learn those habits only slowly, while the arms crisis ripens and bursts overnight. It is uncertain whether a peace based on common endeavor will prove more reliable than one based on formal alliances. Such a peace may reduce the likelihood of wars, but wars may still come. An ideology of world community may or may not develop. The decline of the impenetrable nation-state is a prerequisite to the growth of world community, but there is no guarantee that world community will be achieved. Certainly, peace-keeping machinery and the apparatus of deterrence must be retained and strengthened.

In a world of contingency and paradox, what the future holds for man depends upon his wisdom, his will, his charity, and the choices he makes in his collective behavior.

Notes

[1] The ability of one country to take over another by subversion does not mean that the former nation necessarily has the capacity to administer the country that it has taken over. A nation might bite off more than it could chew or digest.

[2] Most of the smaller nations will not be aggressively inclined, of course, and will have a perspective on informal attack quite different from that of the aggressive nations. They will view the techniques of informal attack as offering additional ways in which their internal affairs can be tampered with. They must fear not only outright aggression but subversion as well.

CHAPTER VII

Military Intervention by the Great Powers: The Rules of the Game

Since its birth, the nation-state system has been characterized by periodic military interventions by the great powers. Yet the phenomenon of intervention has received very little systematic attention. Individual cases of intervention have been examined and have usually been lamented, but there has not been much concern for the identification of regularities in interventionist behavior. This paper examines military interventions by the two great powers—the United States and the Soviet Union—since the end of World War II.[1]

Nations that are a part of an international system must produce norms and doctrines that justify the system and the way that it operates. The central doctrine supporting the system is, of course, that of "national sovereignty," whereby each nation-state is deemed to be sovereign and obedient to no authority beyond itself. Anything that interferes with sovereignty would tend to undermine the foundations of the system. Thus intervention of one nation-state in the affairs of another represents a clear denial of the principle of national sovereignty. If sovereignty is regarded as "good," as it is, then intervention must obviously be regarded as "bad."

The norm of nonintervention is a stabilizing factor on the international scene. The two predominant powers have frequently proclaimed their attachment to the principle of nonintervention. As that principle is currently conceived, however, it is evidently not one that they can live with in practice.[2] The two great powers intervene in the affairs of other nations in a variety of ways and on a continuing basis.[3] The form of intervention that most clearly contravenes the principle of nonintervention is military intervention, and each of the great powers has resorted to it on occasion.

SPHERES OF INFLUENCE

Under what circumstances would one of the predominant powers engage in military intervention? During the period under study, bipolarity has been a prominent feature of the international system. This has meant, among other things, that each of the predominant powers had its own sphere of influence; that there was frequent competition for the support of countries that were not aligned; and that military intervention by either power would be of interest to the other. During this period interventions frequently had to do with the maintenance of extension of one or the other of the spheres of influence.

This raises the question of how spheres of influence are established, how they change, and how their extent is determined. The boundaries of a sphere are tested by probes from the challenging power, in a variety of forms —overt, covert, political, economic, cultural, or military, of which the last is the most dangerous. A probe can be countered by a response on the part of the nation whose sphere is being probed, through a pledge, a threat, a promise, military action, economic aid, and so on.

Probes are the equivalent of test cases in law. They determine the credibility of the claims to a sphere of influence. If probes are not met firmly in a given area a question is automatically raised as to whether that area should still be considered as within a sphere of influence. If the probes are firmly rebuffed, however, rebuff serves to establish, or to reconfirm, the boundaries of a sphere of influence. Khrushchev's effort to locate ballistic missiles in Cuba probed the determination of the United States to maintain its sphere of interest around Cuba, which the powerful American response affirmed. If the United States had not responded firmly to that probe, the entire notion of the Western Hemisphere as an American sphere of influence might have collapsed.

A great power may reconfirm the features of its sphere of influence by actions that it initiates as well as by its response to probes. The American intervention in the Dominican Republic is an example of such an action. The Soviet invasion of Hungary (1956) and Czechoslovakia (1968) confirmed these countries' position in the Soviet sphere. The ability of the Soviet Union to extract from the Rumanian Government an agreement to allow Soviet troops to conduct military maneuvers on its soil reconfirms the location of Rumania within the Soviet sphere.

A nation-state can use a probe to challenge the sphere of influence of another power and to incorporate an area into its own sphere. If one of the great powers extends a series of probes into an uncommitted country, and if those probes are not rebuffed by that country or by the other great power, then it may be considered to have brought that country into its own sphere of interest. For example, if the Soviet Union extended probes into Austria that were not rebuffed by Austria and the Western nations, Austria's position as an uncommitted country would soon be questioned. To be sure, the status of a country is not always clear-cut and a country may be moved into or out of a sphere of influence by degrees.

A sphere of influence can never be said to have been established once and for all. As we said above, a given area remains within a sphere of influence only as long as the dominant nation in that sphere rebuffs probes or reconfirms its sphere by its own initiatives. If a sphere is not maintained, it ceases to be accepted as a sphere by some other power. If an area is known to be in a given sphere of influence and there are no indications that the dominant power has weakened, that area may not be probed very often. A sphere of influence may be regarded as stabilized when 1) the defending power will respond firmly and reliably to probes and 2) when the other power understands that the first will do so.

The norm of nonintervention, to the extent that it actually is a factor in discouraging intervention, helps to stabilize existing spheres of influence. The response to a probe also is a stabilizing factor. The probe itself, however, is an instrument of change. In this perspective the concept of a "sphere of influence" becomes dynamic rather than static. Over a sufficiently long span of time a sphere of influence can take shape, undergo change, and suffer eventual dissolution. The concept of a "sphere of influence" thus has an obvious utility for the analyst of international politics but because of its static appearance, it has proved resistant to effective use.

If one of the great powers should consider setting aside the principle of nonintervention in favor of a military action in some country, that would not mean that its behavior was moving from the realm of the understandable into the realm of the totally unpredictable. There are certain "rules of the game" pertaining to intervention that the great powers are likely to observe, thus giving their behavior a degree of predictability.

The norm contains an *ethical* element since that which is thought to be helpful to the international system is viewed as "good" and behavior which interferes with its workings is deemed to be wicked. The rules of the game, on the other hand, reflect the *interests* of the great powers. The rules have not been established by an external authority, or formally agreed upon; there is simply tacit agreement concerning their substance. They are not invariably followed, but if they are at all, it is because they are simple and appear to accord with the interests of each nation.

The rules of the game are not fixed but evolve over time with changing circumstances. They are made and unmade by the players as they play. A rule that is not agreed upon by both players is no rule at all. Periods of rapid change, therefore, are dangerous because there is an uncertainty concerning the substance of the rules and the way in which the great powers will apply them. The rules of the game are accepted by the two active countries in the subsystem as the intervention rules for the system. Since these rules are the rules of a special subsystem they need not accord with the formulations of international law or the rules applying to other subsystems. Indeed, it is likely that the rules the super-powers abide by in their interventionary behavior may be distasteful to other nations.[4]

I will examine three types of military intervention by the great powers. "Intra-bloc intervention" refers to military intervention by a great power in its own sphere of influence. "Inter-bloc intervention" involves military intervention by one of the great powers in an area that is within the sphere of influence of the other great power. "Extra-bloc intervention" involves intervention by a great power in an area that is not in its sphere of influence or in the sphere of influence of the other power.

Analytically these three types of intervention are clear-cut and distinct, almost ideal types. In practice, however, it is not always easy to fit a concrete example of intervention neatly into one or the other of the categories.

INTRA-BLOC INTERVENTION

The most important rule to be followed by a nation that it is intervening in its own sphere of influence is to act in such a way as to minimize the danger of a direct confrontation with the other great power and to facilitate the power's acceptance of the action. In order to minimize the danger of great power confrontation, there are a number of subordinate rules that the intervening nation is likely to observe.

1. In its pronouncements it will minimize the extent of the intervention.

2. It will minimize the precedent-breaking nature of the action. In an interview at the time of the Dominican Republic intervention, for example, Secretary Rusk denied that the intervention represented "a departure from long-established policy."

3. All pronouncements will stress the temporary and short-term nature of the intervention. Again intervention in the Dominican Republic can be cited.

4. The intervening nation will try to arrange to be invited to intervene by the government of the country in which the intervention is to take place. If the power has been invited in, intervention presumably ceases to be intervention and becomes a friendly act of assistance. The United States was invited to intervene in the Dominican Republic and the Soviet Union arranged to be invited into Hungary. The Soviet Government initially claimed to have been invited to send troops into Czechoslovakia as well.

5. The intervening country will try to achieve a speedy victory. Because the political costs associated with a large-scale military intervention are very little greater than those associated with a small-scale intervention, the intervening power should employ sufficient military force to do the job quickly and thoroughly. The reason for the emphasis on speed is obvious: If fighting is prolonged the behavior of other nations becomes less predictable. They may find it difficult to avoid the temptation to become politically involved. A quick kill, however, presents other nations with a *fait accompli*. The Soviet intervention in Czechoslovakia accords with this rule, for an estimated (by Western sources) 650,000 troops were involved. The Soviet Union apparently

learned the lesson of too little and too late during the first phase of its military intervention in Hungary. The United States injected approximately 35,000 troops into the tiny Dominican Republic.

6. To give the appearance of legitimacy to its intervention the intervening country may try to associate other countries in its sphere of influence with the interventionist action. The Soviet Union arranged to have its troops accompanied by the troops of four other Warsaw Pact countries during its invasion of Czechoslovakia. After its intervention in the Dominican Republic the United States sought, and received, endorsement of this action by the Organization of American States.

If the great power involved feels that it can avoid military intervention, it will probably seek to do so. The use of nonmilitary means of intervention makes it easier to disguise the element of coercion involved and is a far less obvious and disagreeable type of action. Military intervention is the most obvious form of intervention, and it does not leave the other great power the option of minimizing it or ignoring it. The Soviet Union has been "intervening" in the internal affairs of Czechoslovakia since before the coup in 1948, and the prolongation of the intervention had generated something akin to legitimacy. If the Soviet Union had been able to reestablish its control over the country without relying upon troops, the event would have been lamented, and the Soviet Union would have been castigated but Soviet action would have produced far less concern abroad.

The rules noted above apply to the intervening nation. There are also rules to be observed by the other great power.

7. When a great power is confronted with military intervention by the other great power in the latter's sphere of influence, it will express moral outrage and will take various symbolic actions such as

offering resolutions in international bodies.

8. It may consider a variety of relatively mild actions designed to embarass or punish the offending nation for its action.

9. It will not treat the action as a *casus belli.* Neither of the great powers is prepared to go to war over actions that the other takes in its own sphere of influence. Each recognizes that developments in the other's sphere are far more important to the other nation than to it and that the other nation is therefore prepared to run greater risks than it is in connection with those developments. This means that intra-bloc interventions will normally be unilateral rather than competitive, as was the case when Russia intervened in East Germany, Hungary, and Czechoslovakia, and the United States intervened in the Dominican Republic.

INTER-BLOC INTERVENTION

The central rule of the game in the case of inter-bloc intervention is simple and clear-cut: Do not intervene, if you want to avoid war. The logic is an extension of the rules applied in an intra-bloc situation. That is, a nation does not respond militarily to the initiatives of the other power in the sphere of influence of that power and it does not undertake military initiatives in the sphere of the other. This rule is obvious to both powers and will probably be ignored only in the case of a misunderstanding or if the challenging power is purposely leading to war. The United States did not respond militarily to the Soviet interventions in Hungary and Czechoslovakia because it recognized the danger of war. The same realization points to the avoidance of any military initiative by the United States in the Soviet sphere of influence.

Because the rule forbids military intervention in the sphere of the other there are not many examples of such

intervention to be cited. The Soviet effort to locate ballistic missiles in Cuba is an exception and apparently
arose out of a misunderstanding. Because the United
States allowed a pro-Soviet government to exist in Cuba
and did not follow through and overwhelm Cuba at the
time of the Bay of Pigs incident, Khrushchev appears to
have concluded that President Kennedy was not prepared
to maintain the American sphere of interest by strong
action. There an effort to establish a missile basis in Cuba
seemed to him to be a reasonable probe—offering potentially great gains and not involving commensurate risks.
When Khrushchev was persuaded to ignore the rule
against military intervention in the sphere of influence of
the other power he precipitated what was possibly the
most direct and tense showdown between the Soviet
Union and the United States since the end of World War
II.

Khrushchev did not understand that the United States
might hesitate to intervene militarily in its own sphere of
interest and yet be perfectly clear in its mind that it could
not tolerate the military intervention of another power in
that sphere. The United States was not ready to act officially against Cuba in an intra-bloc situation but it was
instantly ready to act when the Soviet missile initiative
created an inter-bloc situation. Instead of applying the
rules pertaining to intra-bloc intervention, President
Kennedy was forced to apply the rules pertaining to inter-
bloc intervention. A great power can choose to intervene
or not to intervene in its own sphere but, unless it is prepared to watch the dissolution of its sphere, it cannot fail
to respond to the military intervention of the other power
in its sphere. President's Kennedy's speech of October 22,
1962 made it clear that Soviet intervention "in an area
well known to have a special and historical relationship
to the United States" was a deliberately provocative and
unjustified change in the status quo which cannot be
accepted by this country, if our courage and our commitments are ever to be trusted again by either friend or foe.

EXTRA-BLOC INTERVENTION

Extra-bloc intervention covers a broad spectrum of cases, everything from intervention in a country that is thoroughly detached from either bloc to intervention in a country that has a special relationship with one of the powers even though it is not in the sphere of influence of that power. The rules are ambiguous.

10. The more important a great power deems an uncommitted area to be, the more seriously it will regard military intervention in that area by the other power. An area may be considered important to a great power because of what that area can add to the great power's strength or because of the necessity of denying the support of that area to the other great power.

11. The more closely an uncommitted area is associated with a sphere of influence the less likely it is that the other great power will take serious offense at the first power's military intervention in that area. That is, the second power perceives the situation as being almost an intra-bloc situation and is therefore prepared to act in almost the way that it would act in an intra-bloc situation.

12. The more closely an uncommitted area is associated with a given sphere of influence the greater will be the concern of that power if the other power should attempt a military intervention. That is, it perceives the situation as similar to the inter-bloc situation and it reacts in a somewhat similar way.

There is obviously a vast grey area between situations that are "almost" intra-bloc and those that are "almost" inter-bloc, and the opportunity for dangerously divergent perceptions by the great powers is great. One of the great powers might regard a third country as almost in its sphere of influence and therefore be prepared to act with the freedom appropriate to an intra-bloc situation. The other great nation might perceive the third nation as uncommitted or in *its* sphere of influence. For example, for geographical and historical reasons, the Soviet Union feels that Yugoslavia is within its sphere of influence. Following the NATO ministerial meeting in November, 1968, however, Secretary Rusk announced that Yugoslavia and Austria fall within the Western sphere of security interests. (Marshal Tito responded by stating that Yugoslavia was not in anyone's sphere of influence and, indeed, did not recognize such spheres.) Given such varying perceptions of Yugoslavia's position, the possibility of a dangerous confrontation is substantial. The danger of a military confrontation between the great powers is not great in intra-bloc situations since the rules are clear and each nation knows what is expected of it. In extra-bloc situations, however, neither may know what to expect of the other.

Several of the intra-bloc rules also apply in extra-bloc cases. For example, if at all possible the intervening country will try to arrange to be invited to intervene, as was the United States in Lebanon in 1958. The intervening nation will want to stress the temporary and special nature of the intervention, and will want to complete the military part of the operation as quickly as possible in order to hold down the level of risk.

THE DECISION TO INTERVENE

The rules of the game may permit a nation to intervene in a given case but they do not command it to do so. What kind of calculations might decision-makers make as they consider the merits of intervention?

Governments will normally consider, as best they can, the costs and gains associated with the proposed intervention. In a given situation there may be a number of different intervention options to be considered, each with a set of benefits and a set of costs associated with it. The decision-makers would have to assess the probable costs of intervention, the probable benefits of intervention, the probable costs of nonintervention, the probable benefits of nonintervention. That is, they would have to calculate the probable *net* benefits (or losses) to be derived from intervention and the probable *net* benefits (or losses) to be derived from nonintervention, which should indicate *whether* the decision should be made for or against intervention. Changes in these values over time must also be incorporated to indicate *when* intervention should or should not occur. When the element of time is incorporated the variety of the possible relationships become apparent. A favorable cost balance now may be reversed some time later, and vice versa. Decision-makers will not find it easy to make calculations of this kind, however, for costs and benefits cannot be quantified with any great precision. Nevertheless it would be possible for them to think in general terms about the relationships between costs and benefits.

To say that the rules of the game are observed because they incorporate elements of self-interest means that these rules must be justifiable in terms of the costs and benefits that would be derived from adherence to them. Why, for example, should an intervening nation seek a clean, quick kill? Because this course of action is likely to minimize long-term costs, for costs associated with intervention increase with the passage of time. Why should a nation try to arrange to be invited to intervene? Because this would cut the costs and risks associated with the intervention. Why should a great power not respond militarily to military intervention by the other power in its own sphere for interest? Because the benefits from the action might be slight and the costs might be great.

A rough cost/benefit analysis can be applied to decisions by the United States and the Soviet Union to intervene militarily in other countries. The decision to intervene will turn on the analysis of the following factors: 1) the existing situation; 2) its seriousness (i.e., present costs); 3) probable future seriousness (i.e., future costs); 4) the policy options available and the effectiveness of each option; 5) present and/or future costs and benefits associated with the use of each option. These factors can be used to analyse the Soviet decision in Czechoslovakia and elsewhere in Eastern Europe.

First, the Soviet Union is willing to tolerate policy deviation on the part of an Eastern European country as long as that deviation does not endanger Soviet control of the Communist Party, the government, and basic governmental policy in that country. In Hungary in 1956 and in East Germany in 1953, the Party/government apparatus could no longer control events in the country. In Czechoslovakia in 1968 the Party/government apparatus *would* no longer follow Soviet direction. It is loss of control of the situation by the Soviet Union that leads to the question of intervention being raised.

Next to be considered is the estimate of the seriousness of the situation. Loss of control in a country does not automatically bring military intervention. For several years the Soviet Union lacked adequate control over the policies of the Rumanian Government, yet did not intervene militarily in Rumania. The explanation for the failure of the Soviet Union to act probably lies in the calculation by Soviet leaders that Rumania's defection was not proving very costly. It is noteworthy that the Rumanian Government acted in a careful and circumspect way and did not actively encourage other governments to follow its example. That is, the Rumanian Government was careful not to increase the costs of its defection to the Soviet Union, and Soviet leaders apparently concluded that the benefits of disciplinary action against Rumania did not offset its costs.

The third factor involves the probable future costs of a defection. In the Hungarian and Czechoslovak cases the situation was not stabilized but was undergoing progressive deterioration. In the Czechoslovak case, for example, Soviet and other Eastern European leaders were concerned not only with events in Czechoslovakia but with the impact of the Czechoslovak events on Eastern Europe as a whole. On May 8, 1968, East German, Polish, and Bulgarian Communist leaders met with Soviet leaders in Moscow to discuss the implications of the events in Czechoslovakia, doubtless concerned with the problem of contagion or of a "demonstration effect."

The Soviet leaders probably understood that the present and future costs associated with intervention would be substantial. For example, it would make clearer the true relationship between the Soviet Union and its Eastern European clients. The hollowness of the claim of independence and the emptiness of the non-intervention pledges in the Warsaw Pact would be made evident. Intervention would also have an impact upon Communist Parties around the world, might create further cleavages in Eastern Europe, and might encourage the Western countries to pursue more active military policies in NATO. Nevertheless, from the Soviet point of view, the costs of nonintervention were increasing daily and a process of bloc disintegration may have appeared to have been under way. In the end the Soviet leaders concluded that the net benefits of intervention were greater than those of nonintervention. The rapidly rising costs of nonintervention doubtless placed a premium on action at the earliest possible moment.

Fourth, is a consideration of the available policy options and the costs and benefits associated with each. If there were political and economic control techniques available to the Soviet Union they would doubtless be considered before military intervention would be undertaken. In the cases under consideration, however, the non-military control techniques had already proved ineffective and the situation was no longer under control. Military intervention probably appeared as the means of last resort. It had one great advantage: it provided an assured means for reestablishing firm control. Under the umbrella afforded by military intervention a new set of controls could be instituted in the country in which intervention took place.

Finally, there is the impact of the passage of time on the costs and benefits associated with each policy option. Military intervention, for example, might cost more (or less) at a later date than it would at the present moment.

Because intervention is costly, neither great power will intervene in its own sphere of interest for casual reasons. Each has a threshold of toleration and will take military action only when that threshold is passed. There was some Soviet military intervention in Cuba before the missile crisis, but the United States chose not to make an issue of it. When the Russians landed missiles that readily threatened the United States, however, it did intervene. The location of a threshold is not fixed once and for all but varies with circumstances. For example, because of its experience with Fidel Castro in Cuba, the United States became more concerned about the threat of Communism in Latin America. At the time of the disturbances in the Dominican Republic, therefore, the United States government acted swiftly and with overwhelming force, as if to say, "There shall be no more Castros in this hemisphere." At a time, before Castro came to power, the equivalent level of provocation might have produced nothing more than official warnings and reproaches.

Once the decision to intervene has been made, justification is not a significant problem. There is probably no intervention so outrageous that a great power will not be able, in short order, to develop a flattering justification for it. After the intervention in Czechoslovakia Soviet ideologues soon launched the doctrine of the "Socialist community." Thus *Pravda*, on September 25, 1968 published the statement that

> [each Communist party] is responsible not only to its own people, but also to all the socialist countries, to the entire Communist movement. As a social system, world socialism is the common gain of the working people of all lands; it is indivisible and its defense is

the common cause of all Communists and all progressives in the world, in the first place, the working folk of the socialist countries.

Naturally the Communists of the fraternal countries could not allow the socialist states to be inactive in the name of an abstractly understood sovereignty, when they saw that the country stood in peril of antisocialist degeneration.

There is no doubt that the actions of the five allied socialist countries in Czechoslovakia directed to the vital interests of the socialist community, and the sovereignty of socialist Czechoslovakia first and foremost, will be increasingly supported by all those who have the interest of the present revolutionary movement, of peace and security of peoples, of democracy and socialism at heart.

People who "disapprove" of the actions of the allied socialist states are ignoring the decisive fact that these countries are defending the interests of all, of world socialism, of the entire world revolutionary movement.[5]

The concept of a "threshold of toleration" can be spelled out in terms of a nation's cost/benefits analysis. A nation will intervene when the net benefits (i.e., benefits minus costs) of intervention are greater than the net benefits of non-intervention. It is easy to see that the location of this point will vary as the inputs into the cost-benefits analysis change.

The Monroe Doctrine offers a reasonably precise statement of the basic rule of the game for inter-bloc situations. In his Seventh Annual Message to Congress (1823) President Monroe asserted "that the American continents, by the free and independent condition which they have assumed and maintain, are henceforth not to be considered as subjects for future colonization by any European powers."

The so-called "Roosevelt Corollary" to the Monroe Doctrine asserts the basic right rule of the game for intra-bloc situations, that is, the right of the predominant power to intervene in its own sphere of influence. Theodore Roosevelt, in his Annual Message in 1904, stated:

> Chronic wrongdoing,or an impotence which results in a general loosening of the ties of civilized society, may in America, as elsewhere, ultimately require intervention by some civilized nation, and in the Western Hemisphere the adherence of the United States to the Monroe doctrine may force the United States, however reluctantly, in flagrant cases of such wrongdoing or impotence, to the exercise of an international police power.

Both the Soviet Union and the United States have also developed serviceable doctrines to justify covert or overt intervention in uncommitted countries. The Soviet Union intervenes in order to support "wars of liberation" against foreign or domestic oppressors. The United States finds sufficient justification for its actions in the necessity of resisting the varied threats of Communist tyranny and preserving democracy. This reasoning is the same as that used by the United States to explain hemispheric actions such as the intervention in the Dominican Republic, Guatemala, and the Bay of Pigs.

Discussions of deterrence have usually centered around the possibility of nuclear attack. It is obvious however that the basic concept of deterrence can have wider application. One nation's effort to deter military action by the other need not be confined to a possible nuclear exchange but can extend to military intervention of the kinds discussed above.

While the concept of deterrence can be applied to each of the three types of great power military intervention, its utility varies with each type. In the case of inter-bloc intervention, the defending nation rarely has much of a problem in deterring attack, for the rules of the game are so clear-cut and intervention is so manifestly dangerous that no deterrent action is likely to be necessary. The basic structure of the situation provides the necessary deterrent.

Intra-bloc intervention presents quite a different deterrent problem. How is one nation to deter the other from intervening militarily in its own sphere of influence? Here also the rules of the game provide the basic framework within which attempts at deterrence must operate. These rules place an upper limit on the kind of credible threats a nation can make in trying to deter the other, since the basic rule of the game in the case of inter-bloc intervention is that the other will not deem intervention to be a *casus belli*. For example, if the United States were considering intervening militarily in Cuba it would not regard a Soviet threat of war as credible. Nor were the threats that emerged from the November, 1968, NATO meetings aimed at deterring a possible Soviet military intervention in Rumania; the NATO nations were not in a position to offer guarantees to Eastern European nations against Soviet action and therefore their threats were simply exercises in verbal militance.

There may be other ways to deter an attack. The deterring nation can make non-military threats, including threats directed toward targets other than the offending nation. The United States could scarcely threaten war in order to deter Soviet military action against an eastern Europe nation, but it might indicate that such action would hinder the achievement of Soviet-American detente, would lead to the cancellation of specific forms of collaboration, would lead to economic reprisals, and would cause the United States to take increased measures for military preparedness for other eventualities.

In addition, officials in the deterring nation should keep their minds open to the possibility of including positive inducements in its deterrent program. The objective of the defending nation is to alter the intentions of the other nation and inducements as well as threats may contribute to that end. There are many matters on which the two great powers share a common concern, and there are always actions that one *wants* the other to take (concerning trade, arms control, the United Nations, the two Germanies, China, and alliance policy, among others) as well as actions that it does *not want* the other to take.

The deterrent actions that the defending nation takes,

along with any inducements it offers, will be fed into the cost/benefit calculations of the other nation. If the decision to intervene is hanging in the balance this collection of deterrents and inducements may prove decisive. On the other hand, if the threatening nation is strongly inclined to go ahead with the intervention, these deterrents and inducements will probably be insufficient to alter the balance. In many cases the deterrent program will be of marginal significance; in the case of inter-bloc intervention special deterrent actions are usually unnecessary in the case of intra-bloc intervention these actions are often unavailing.

The prospects for deterrence are more hopeful in the case of extra-bloc intervention. For one thing the stakes involved are likely to be smaller. National security will probably not be involved as it might be in the other two cases. The greater the potential gains from an intervention the greater the risks and costs the threatening nation will be prepared to bear. The smaller the potential gains, the smaller will be the costs and risks that it will be willing to bear and the more easily those gains can be offset by a program of deterrents. As in the case of intra-bloc intervention, the defending nation will want to consider both inducements and deterrents in trying to alter the intentions of the threatening nation; it should not confine its attention to the immediate area in contention but should range about widely. For example, if the United States were trying to deter a Soviet military intervention in the Middle East it should not focus on that area alone but should consider the deterrents and inducements open to it in connection with the United Nations, Western Europe, Eastern Europe, Southeast Asia, technical collaboration, and so on.

The deterring nation must determine: 1) what threats to make (or inducements to offer); 2) how to make those threats credible; 3) whether it will back up those threats in the event that the other nation is not deterred by them. The question of bluff is separable from the question of credibility. The first has to do with the intent of the deterring state; the second has to do with the perceptions of the intervening state. Bruce Russett has examined the factors that help establish the credibility of threats designed to deter interventions. After examining seventeen cases, he observes,

> the credibility of deterrence depends upon the economic, political and military interdependence of pawn and defender. Where visible ties of commerce, past or present political integration, or military cooperation exist, an attacker will be much more likely to bow before the defender's threat—or if he does not bow, he will very probably find himself at war with the defender. . . . Under these circumstances the effectiveness of the defender's threat is heavily dependent on the tangible and intangible bonds between him and the pawn. If other factors are equal, an attacker will regard a military response by the defender as more probable the greater the number of military, political, and economic ties between pawn and defender.[6]

This suggests that the deterring nation might give added credibility to threats by strengthening the bonds between itself and the third country (the pawn). For example, it can send military aid and advisors to the third nation.[7] Such actions would demonstrate its stake in the other country.

In addition, the nation trying to deter intervention must obviously be able to perform the threatened action. If the capability does not exist, the threat automatically loses all credibility. Credibility will also be increased if the nation making a threat stands to suffer substantial losses if it fails to back up its threat. The credibility of a threat is also influenced by the way in which the state considering intervention perceives the interests of the defending state. If one state says to another, "Attack us and we shall strike back with the means at our disposal," the threat will be credible, for such retaliation will be in keeping with the attacking nation's conception of the defender's interests. If one says, "Attack some other nation and we shall strike at you with all the means at our disposal," the threat is apt to be less credible. The attacker would be inclined to ask skeptically, "Do they really care that much about this other country?" If the attacker does not feel that the defending country's interests are deeply involved with the third country, it will perceive the defender's threat as disproportionate and lacking in credibility. Yet there is still room for misunderstanding. The defender might feel that, the third state is not intrinsically of vital importance, the consequences of letting the attacker's aggression go unchecked would be very serious. The way that the defending country perceives its interests is far different from the way that the attacker believes that it perceives those interests, and the stage is set for conflict.

Notes

[1] The author wishes to thank the graduate students in his seminar on international politics for their interest in discussing the ideas that appear in this paper and for their important contribution to the analysis that the paper offers.

[2] See the author's *The Functioning of the International Political System* (New York, Macmillan, 1967), Chapters 13 and 16.

[3] It ought to be noted that this intervention, in such forms as economic aid, technical assistance, military assistance, is often sought by the country in which the "intervention" takes place.

[4] It should be emphasized that when an observer refers to the "rules of the game" for intervention he is not signifying approval of intervention nor adopting an immoral stance. He is acting as a social scientist rather than a moralist and is seeking to analyze and understand rather than to pass judgment.

[5] The full text reprinted in *The New York Times*, September 27, 1968.

[6] "The Calculus of Deterence," *The Journal of Conflict Resolution* (Vol. VII, No. 2), June 1963, pp. 103, 106.

[7] "In every case where the defender went to war he had previously sent military advisors and arms to the pawn." *Ibid.*

CHAPTER VIII

Nonintervention and

Conditional Intervention

As has been seen, the doctrine of nonintervention is closely related to the idea of national sovereignty. If each nation-state is viewed as independent, self-sufficient, its own source of law and right, and owing obedience to no other nation, intervention can have no legal or moral justification. Nonintervention is an obvious corollary of national sovereignty.

Both ideas—national sovereignty and nonintervention—were formed during an earlier era and belong to the past. For example, the doctrine of nonintervention assumes that nations respect the territorial integrity of other nations and that there are no gross disparities in wealth, strength, and viability. It likewise assumes that the techniques of informal penetration have not yet been developed and that less developed nations are not seeking assistance from the more developed nations. The relations of actors in the international system have changed markedly since World War I; the basic doctrines associated with the nation-state system have changed little.

The decline in the relative inviolability of individual nation-states, noticeable during the interwar years, has been far more pronounced since the end of World War II.[1] Associated with this decline has been the rapid increase in the number of techniques available to nations and international organizations for the penetration of target nations.

Formal government-to-government relations between nations allow only for the application of external pressure. They do not enable the administrative agencies of one country to reach inside another country in an effort to bring about desired change. The techniques of informal access, on the other hand, are distinguished by precisely this capacity and that explains the increase in their number and importance. These techniques include information programs, cultural exchange programs, many kinds of economic aid, technical assistance in many forms, military training missions, military civic action programs, political warfare, economic warfare, psychological warfare, and the organization of insurgency and internal warfare. Almost any form of transfer of resources, skills, or knowledge from one national society to another can be made a basis for informal penetration.

The doctrine of nonintervention stands in serious need of modification. Powerful nations do not, and cannot, adhere to it. They cannot adhere to it *and* offer leadership because the exercise of international leadership often involves intervention. The United States, for example, cannot assist a poor nation along the path of development while observing the principle of nonintervention because a full-scale program of assistance revolves around various forms of intervention. One nation cannot help another nation modernize and, at the same time, cling to the time-honored principle of nonintervention.

When the United States offers "technical assistance" to a country this assistance may involve advice on legislation, legal procedures, social structure, land tenure, and policy toward unions and other nongovernmental organizations. Its economic aid, and the advice associated with that aid, may involve changes in export policy, the pattern of savings and investment, the balance of agriculture and industry, the distribution of wealth, the services available in the society, and the political and economic power of various segments in the society. The encouragement of family planning may alter long-standing social patterns, and industrial development may tend to produce secular attitudes that undermine established religious beliefs. Congress has instructed the Agency for International Development to design its programs so as to contribute to the development of democratic institutions in countries receiving aid. Certainly school self-help programs, literacy programs, and the training of administrators and political leaders cannot fail to have an impact on politics in the host nation. When American officers train indigenous military forces in riot control or improve the quality of those military forces, they are taking actions that may affect political stability and modify the future political and military development of the country. In short, the actions of a deeply involved donor nation may leave few aspects of the national life of a host country untouched.

The stronger nations do not adhere to the principle of nonintervention and weaker nations do not desire strict adherence. The seeming paradox disappears as soon as it is realized that intervention is not always bad and nonintervention is not always good. The poorer nations, standing in great need of assistance, cannot afford to have the wealthy nations adhere strictly to the principle of nonintervention.

Since the stronger nations do not adhere to the principle of nonintervention when it does not please them to do so, and since the weaker nations do not want the principle to be strictly observed, it would seem that the principle should have receded into irrelevance and have ceased to be of any practical concern. However, while the principle of nonintervention has not been strong enough to prevent the development of techniques of informal access, such as economic aid and cultural exchange, it has been strong enough to hamper their development and impede efficient administration. Organizations find it difficult to do well those things that they are not certain they should be doing at all. Because "intervention" is commonly presumed to be bad, those engaging in it must cope with a public relations problem. Over the years they have found it helpful to emphasize the "technical" and "economic" aspects of assistance programs rather than their social, political, and military aspects.[2] It is one thing to get around the principle of nonintervention in practice; it would be quite another for a government to criticize the principle openly or to note its ambiguities. Circumvention, therefore, is accompanied by doctrinal lip-service.

Is it time to dispense with the concept of nonintervention altogether? Should it be replaced by something else? The answer must hinge on an understanding of the function that the doctrine of nonintervention has performed. It is one of a handful of principles that has been used to govern the relations of nations in the international system. It has helped to protect weak nations by defining as illegitimate the interventionist actions of the strong. If the less developed nations cannot afford to have the principle of nonintervention rigidly followed by the wealthy nations at present, neither should they rejoice in seeing the principle set aside.

Three points seem clear: first, the principle of nonintervention is obsolete; second, it has fulfilled a useful and important function; third, there is nothing else that quite takes its place. It cannot survive in its present form, yet it cannot be allowed to perish. This line of analysis suggests that the concept should be redefined, if that is possible, so that it becomes viable once again and can serve as a restraint upon the powerful nations in their dealings with less powerful nations. This chapter, having indicated the need for doctrinal revision, will attempt to suggest a basis for such revision.

The doctrine is no longer useful because it is too absolute in its accepted form. A principle that condemns all intervention is not a useful concept and must be set aside. If a new doctrine is to be developed it must take account of some of the salient facts of international life and it must assert that *intervention is sometimes a positive good*. Intervention can be good or bad, depending on the nature of the intervention and the circumstances in which it takes place, and this must be the basis of any new doctrine pertaining to intervention. Intervention should neither be condemned nor endorsed without qualification.

The principle of unconditional nonintervention must be replaced by one of conditional intervention. This principle would be based upon twin realizations: first, that intervention is often legitimate and may be badly needed; second, that all intervention must operate under constraint. A code is needed which will give effect to this general principle and will reflect the interests of both donor and host. It should indicate the conditions under which intervention would be legitimate and the conditions under which it would not be legitimate.

Donor nations and host nations alike would benefit from the development of such a code. The host nation would benefit from the explicit recognition that it was justified in seeking safeguards against undue foreign influence on its domestic processes and in objecting to certain arrangements proposed by donor nations. Donor nations would benefit because the code would approve certain kinds of intervention and, by so doing, would legitimize them.

The wealthy nations of the world must be persuaded to allocate a greater percentage of their resources to foreign aid but they are not likely to do so if they must continually defend their well-meaning actions against foreign charges of interventionism and neocolonialism. Neither are they likely to increase the level of foreign aid significantly while there is division at home over the justifiability of aid programs. In the United States, Congressmen and others have expressed concern over what seemed to them to be the quasi-imperialist quality of the political purposes sometimes associated with U.S. aid programs. A code of fair play would help reduce these misgivings by drawing a line between the acceptable and the unacceptable. The code would recognize as legitimate the desire of the donor nation to have a degree of supervision over the programs that it is financing and would specify the procedures that are (or are not) appropriate to the achievement of such supervision. At present it is often difficult for the donor nation to overcome the anxieties of the host nation and to convince it that the donor nation has no designs on it. The donor might find it easier to set the host nation at ease if it could state that it fully accepted the provisions of the code of intervention and intended to be guided by the code in all respects.

The code would make it easier for both donor and host to behave responsibly and to be protected against irresponsible attack. Because the realities of the situation are not widely understood at present, it is easy for irresponsible elements to compare the ideal of nonintervention with the fact of intervention and thus undermine the position of those who attempt to negotiate agreements. Officials in the host nation are attacked on the ground that they are tools of the donor nation, while officials in the donor nation are attacked on the ground that they are engaging in thinly disguised imperialism.

What factors should be considered by those drawing up a code of intervention? Distinctions should certainly be made concerning the purposes of the donor nation. The extension of economic aid in order to speed the economic development of a host nation is certainly a very different thing from the use of aid as a means of subverting a host nation or its decision-making processes. Some political purposes are acceptable and others are not. For example, it might be appropriate to help a regime consolidate its position so that it could undertake programs of reform, or to help a government overcome a financial crisis that threatened its life. It might not be appropriate, on the other hand, to use an information program in order to undermine a government, to alter the composition of a government, to attack the opposition, or to influence the outcome of an election.

Also relevant to the code would be the purposes of the host nation. The code might approve military assistance for some purposes but rule it out in cases where there was a likelihood that the host government would use the assistance to crush the opposition and perpetuate itself in power.

A consideration of importance would be the mechanics of the relation between host and donor. A great many procedural arrangements are possible and the code could be selective, endorsing some and ruling out others that would give the donor undue influence over decision-making in the host country. For example, a distinction might be drawn between a donor nation's training the nationals of the host country to do certain administrative jobs and actually sending in its own nationals to perform administrative tasks.

Another factor would be the extent to which the host government was informed about the activities of the donor nation inside the host country. Host governments are frequently fearful of the covert operations of secret agencies such as the Central Intelligence Agency. The code might rule out all actions by the donor in a host country about which the donor was not prepared to keep the host government fully and officially informed. A formal pledge on the part of the donor to eschew covert political, military, and economic operations might ease relations between donor and host.

A further consideration in developing the code might be the extent to which the host government desires a given intervention. The code might indicate that no intervention would be deemed legitimate that the host nation, wisely or unwisely, did not want. This rules out a donor's forcing an unwanted form of intervention on a host nation as a condition for receiving another, desired, form of assistance.

A related concern is the relationship between donor

and host and the extent to which the latter is capable of making autonomous decisions. If the host nation is not really free to disapprove of the intervention of the donor then its approval of that intervention is not significant. Another consideration is the stability of the host government and the extent to which it is viewed as legitimate in its own country.

The persons drawing up the code need to be aware of the special sensitivity of questions relating to political and military intervention. The code needs to spell out the circumstances under which one nation might legitimately intervene militarily in the affairs of another nation and when it might not. For example, it might be deemed appropriate to help a nation defend itself against external aggression but not appropriate to give it military aid if it appeared that such aid might be used by the government to maintain itself in office.

It is helpful to think of host/donor agreements as being ranged along a scale that measures the degree of protection afforded to each party in a given agreement. In the figure below, the dotted line indicates the region along this scale in which would fall those arrangements making adequate concessions to the interests of both host and donor and which would therefore be in keeping with the code.

low safeguards for host	Range Approved by Code	high safeguards for host
X	Y	Z
—O—	—O—	—O—
high safeguards for donor		low safeguards for donor

An agreement located at point Y, for example, would fall in the approved range.

The code would offer a starting point for negotiation and would obviate discussion of many issues. It would not, of course, make bargaining and negotiation unnecessary. As a rule, the greater the protection for the donor against the waste and misuse of its resources, the fewer are the safeguards that will be available to the host.[3] Conversely, the greater the protection for the host nation, the fewer will be the safeguards for the donor. In the figure above, an agreement located at point X, to the left of the approved range, would mean that the donor has driven too hard a bargain and that the host nation has too few safeguards. If an agreement were located at point Z to the right of the approved range, it would mean that the host nation had driven too hard a bargain and the donor had settled for less control over its intervention than was deemed desirable by the framers of the code.

In the bargaining prior to an agreement between host and donor, the host nation would try to get agreement as far to the right along the scale as possible, thus giving itself maximum control over the intervention. The donor nation would try to achieve agreement as far to the left as possible in order to increase its control over the resources or skills that it is transferring. If the demands of either party prove to be too extreme, the other would not be willing to pay the price involved and there would be no agreement.

The terms on which host and donor might agree would change with circumstances and with the bargaining strength of each party. If the bargaining relationship were an unequal one, agreement might fall to one side or the other of the approved range. Hopefully, however, the existence of the code would mean that most bargaining would take place within the framework provided by the code. Greater or lesser bargaining strength would still be reflected in the terms of an agreement, but the code would create limits outside of which agreement would not normally be reached. The wealthy and powerful nations might be willing to abide by the terms of the code and adopt it as an "ethic of intervention" even when their bargaining power in a particular situation might enable them to exact terms from the host nation more favorable than those provided for in the code.

The development of a code of intervention is long overdue. Its drafting is a task that should be undertaken by international lawyers, and certainly there is a vast reservoir of practice that could serve as a basis for rules. To be sure, a significant social innovation rarely emerges until there is a widespread and recognized need for it, and there is not at present any such widespread recognition of the need for a code of intervention. On the other hand, there are so many developing nations, and agreements between host nation and donor nation have become so numerous and important that an awareness of the need for a code may come rapidly. If work on such a code were undertaken under the auspices of the United Nations it is possible that by the time significant progress had been made on its drafting the international political environment might have become far more receptive to its adoption.

Notes

[1] See, for example, John Herz, *International Politics in the Atomic Age* (New York: Columbia University Press, 1959) and Richard W. Cottam, *Competitive Interference and Twentieth Century Diplomacy* (Pittsburgh: University of Pittsburgh Press, 1967).

[2] It is worth noting that the same kind of problem has sometimes been encountered by international organizations. The injunction concerning intervention is held to apply to international organizations as well as to individual nation-states. The charters of many organizations prohibit them from intervening in the "domestic" affairs of member nations. Yet, if those organizations are to do the jobs that member nations often want them to do, they *must* intervene in domestic affairs.

[3] See Richard Cottam's discussion of "levels of tolerance" in *Competitive Interference and Twentieth Century Diplomacy* (Pittsburgh: University of Pittsburgh Press, 1967), Chapter I.

Index

Abetz, Otto, 35, 37
Academic Peace Committee, 60
Accessibility: access and, distinction between, 20; concept of, 20-23; substantive, 21-23, 115; technical, 21-23
Action Francaise, 36
AFL-CIO training program, 90
Agency for International Development (AID), 17
Agricultural Trade and Development and Assistance Act (1954), 83
Albania, Communists in, 55, 56
Algeria, Communists in, 64
Alliance for Progress program, 18, 28, 99-107
American Trading Organization (AMTORG), 18
Arab Pioneer Youth of Israel, 60
Arabic-Language Poets, 60
Armed Forces Assistance to Korea, 86
Aski system, 42, 44
Aswan High Dam, 64
"Attack," informal: concept of, 9, 15; disloyalty and, 113-38; ideology and, 123-138; international organizations and, 140-55; loyalty and, 116-38; nation-state system and, 156-76;
    conflict among nations, patterns, of, 157-60; international stability, 160-165; nation-state, nature and functioning of, 168-172; nature and functioning of, 172-76; power in world politics, nature of, 156-57;
Nazi experience, 30-44;
    Austria, 37-39; Czechoslovakia, 33-34, 39-41; eco-

"Attack" (*continued*)
    nomic warfare, 41-44; France, 34-37; South-West Africa, 34; Soviet experience compared with, 66-67;
    Soviet experience, 45-67; China, 53; cultural diplomacy, 62-64; Czechoslovakia, 50, 57-60; economic aid programs, 64-65; foreign policy, 65-66; front organizations, 60-62; Nazi experience compared with, 66-67; Spain, 53-54; technical assistance programs, 64-65;
    United States experience, 69-110;
    Alliance for Progress program, 99-107; covert operations, 91-99; cultural exchange program, 80, 83-84; economic aid program, 73-78, 87-89; foreign policy, 69-70; international organizations, 81-83; Latin America, 69, 72, 78, 81-82, 94, 99-107; military aid program, 73; military civil action program, 85-87; North Atlantic Treaty Organization, 80-81; political development program, 88-91; technical assistance program, 78-80
Auslander-Sonderkonten fur Inlandshazlungen (*aski*), 42
Austria, Nazi penetration of, 37-39
Austrian Legion, 37

Balkans, Nazi economic warfare in, 42-43

Bayer Company, 35, 41
Bay of Pigs, *see* Cuba
Belgium, collaborators in, 114
Benelux Economic Union, 145
Benes, Eduard, 58, 59, 60
Blitzkreig, doctrines of, 32
Bolivia, Nazi economic warfare in, 41
Bolsheviks and Bolshevism, 7, 35, 45, 46, 49, 50, 51
Borodin, Mikhail M., 53
Bosch, Juan, 90
Bradley, General Omar Nelson, 57
Branch plants, foreign, 19
Breton Fascists, 34
Bulgaria, 56, 190

Cambodia, 79
Cartel agreements, 43-44
Castro, Fidel, 71, 91, 94, 125, 191
Central American Common Market (CACM), 145
Central American Economic Cooperation Committee, 144
Central Intelligence Agency (CIA), 17, 83, 89, 91, 98, 99, 108
Chamberlain, Neville, 33-34
Charter of Punta del Este, 104
Chiang Kai-shek, General, 53
Chile, Nazi economic warfare in, 41
China: ideological split with Soviet Union, 64; Soviet informal penetration of, 53, 194
Circle of Friends of Arabic Progressive Literature, 60
Cold War, the, 7, 8, 9, 48, 72, 73, 84, 127
Cold warfare, 3-4, 7-8; activities of, 3; nature of, 3-4
Cominform, *see* Communist Information Bureau
Comintern, *see* Communist International
Comite des Forges, 36
Comite France-Allemagne, 35
Committee for European Economic Cooperation (CEEC), 74
Communism, 14, 65, 66, 123, 129
Communist Information Bureau (Cominform), 56-57

Communist International (Comintern), 7, 31, 49, 51-53, 54
Communist-front organizations, 60-62
Conditional intervention, concept of, 108
Conflict: among nations, patterns of, 157-60; doctrine of, Lenin's, 50
Congo: Communists in, 64; United Nations operation in, 148-50
Counterpart, concept of, 76-77
Counterpenetration, 21
Covert informal penetration, 10-11, 16-17, 91-99
Croix de Feu, 36
Cuba: U.S. intervention in, 91, 92, 93-94, 96-97, 185, 194; Soviet intervention in, 179, 185, 191
Cultural diplomacy, Soviet, 62-64
Cultural exchange programs, 80, 83-84
Cultural exhibitions, 62
Czechoslovakia: Nazi informal penetration of, 33-34, 39-41; Soviet coup in, 50, 51-60; Soviet intervention in, 179, 182, 191-92

Danmark National Socialistika Arbejder Parti, 34
Declaration of Lima (1938), 101
Declaration of Principles of Inter-American Solidarity and Cooperation, 101
Defense Department, U. S., 17, 83
Democratic Lawyers' Association, 60
Detente, Soviet-American, 194
Development Aid Fund, 79
Disloyalty, informal access and, 113-38
Dominican Republic: Organization of American States and, 146-47; United States occupation of, 69; intervention in 179, 182, 191, 193

East Germany, 129, 138, 184, 189

Economic aid programs, 64-65, 73-78, 87-89
Economic warfare, Nazi experience, 41-44
Educational exchange programs, 62-63
Eisenhower, Dwight D., 71, 95, 127
Eisenlohr, German Minister, 39-40
Emerging areas, problems of, 78
Ethiopia, United States civil action program in, 85
European Coal and Steel Community, 14, 76, 142
European Cooperation Administration (ECA), 77
European Economic Community (Common Market), 14, 77, 142
European Recovery Program, 14, 78, 102; see also Marshall Plan
External pressure, 5

Federation of Democratic Women, 60
Fellowship of Reconciliation, 91
"Fifth column" activities, 7
Foreign aid programs, 14-15
Foreign policy: informal penetration and, 11; Soviet Union, 65-66; United States, 69-70
France: collaborators in, 114; Communists in, 55, 56, 57; Nazi informal penetration of, 34-37
Franco-German Society, 35
French Revolution, 8
Fuentes, Miguel Ydigoras, 97
Fulbright-Hays Act (1961), 83

Galen-Bluecher, General, 53
Gaulle, Charles de, 80, 81
Germany, see Nazi
Gillars, Mildred (Axis Sally), 113
Glaise-Horstenau, Austrian Minister of War, 38
Goebbels, Joseph Paul, 36
Goerdeler, Karl Friedrich, 113
Goering, Hermann, 38
Good Neighbor Policy, 69, 93, 94, 100, 105
Gottwald, Clement, 58, 60

Government access, 17, 19
Governmental international organizations, informal access by, 17, 18
Great Britain, United States loan to, 73
Greece: Communists in, 55, 56; United States economic and military aid to, 73
Guatemala: United States civil action program in, 85; United States covert operation in, 93, 95, 193
Guerilla warfare, 50, 56, 71, 85, 87
Guevara, Che, 125
Guinea, Communists in, 64

Haiti, United States occupation of, 69
Hammarskjold, Dag, 148
Hamsun, Knut, 113
Henlein, Conrad, 33, 39, 40, 113
Herz, John, 12-13
Hiss, Alger, 113
Hitler, Adolf, 6, 19, 30-34, 35, 37, 41, 50, 66, 67, 123, 128
Ho Chi Minh, 71
Holland, collaborators in, 114
Hoxha, Enver, 56
Hungary, Communists in, 51; Soviet intervention in, 179, 182, 184, 189

Ideology, informal access and, 123-38
India: Communists in, 64; Soviet informal penetration of, 54
Informal penetration (access), 3-28; covert, 10-11, 16-17, 91-99; disloyalty and, 113-138; foreign policy and, 11, 65-66, 69-70; growth of, 11-12; ideology and, 123-138; informal attack and support, 9, 15; Nazi experience, 30-44; Soviet experience, 45-67; institutionalization of, 10; international organizations and, 140-55; loyalty and, 116-38; modern, as distinguished from historic, 9-11; nation-state system and, 156-176;

Informal penetration (*continued*)
conflict among nations,
patterns of, 157-60; international organizations, role
of, on world scene, 165-68,
173; international stability,
160-65; nation-state, nature
and functioning of, 168-72;
nature and functioning of,
172-176; power in world
politics, nature of, 156-57;
Nazi experience,30-44;
Austria, 37-39; Czechoslovakia, 33-34, 39-41; eco-
nomic warfare, 41-44;
France, 34-37; South-West
Africa, 34; Soviet experience compared with, 66-67;
objectives of, 9; organizational
conquest by, 17, 18, 24, 60-62;
overt, 10-11; participants in,
10; Soviet experience, 45-67;
China, 53; cultural diplomacy, 62-64; Czechoslo-
vakia, 50, 57-60; economic
aid programs, 64-65;
foreign policy, 65-66; front
organizations, 60-62; Nazi
experience compared with,
66-67; Spain, 53-54; technical assistance programs,
64-65;
targets of, 10; techniques of
6-7, 9-10, 23-24; technology
and, 10, 12; types of, 17;
United States experience,
69-110;
Alliance for Progress program, 99-107; covert operations, 91-99; cultural exchange programs, 80, 83-
84; economic aid programs,
73-78, 87-89; foreign policy,
69-70; international organizations, 81-83; Latin
America, 69, 72, 78, 81-82,
94, 99-107; military aid
program, 73; military civil
action programs, 85-87;
North Atlantic Treaty
Organization, 80-81; political development program,
88-91; technical assistance
programs, 78-80; as a
method of conditional inter-

Informal penetration (*continued*)
vention, 198-200
Information programs, 15, 17
Institute for Inter-American
Affairs, 78
Intellectuals, role of, 26-27
Inter-American Commission on
Human Rights, 146
Inter-American Development
Bank, 82
Inter-American Fund for
Special Operations, 82
Internal pressure, 6
International Bank for Recon-
struction and Development
(World Bank), 144
International Development
Association, 144
International Finance Corpora-
tion, 143-44
International Labor Organiza-
tion (ILO), 141, 143
International Monetary Fund,
81, 143
International organizations, *see*
Governmental international
organizations; Organizations,
international
*International Politics in the
Atomic Age* (Herz), 12-13
Intervention: conditional, chapt.
VII; code of, 201-207; mil-
itary, chapt. VII; extra-block,
186-87; inter-block, 184-85;
intra-block, 181-184; cost-
benefit analysis of, 188-92;
deterrence of, 192-97; rules
of, 182-86
Iran, Soviet informal penetration of, 64
Iraq, Communists in, 64
Ireland, Soviet informal penetration of, 54
Israel, Communist-front organizations in, 60
Israel Communist Youth Organization, 60
Israel-Bulgaria Friendship
League, 60
Israel-Czechoslovakia Friendship League, 60
Israel-Polish Friendship League,
60
Israel-USSR Friendship League,
60

Israeli National Committee for Peace, 60
Israeli Peace Movement, 60
Italy, Communists in, 55, 56-57

Japan, Soviet informal penetration of, 54
Java, Soviet informal penetration of, 54
Johnson, Lyndon B., 71

Kasavubu, President of the Congo, 149
Kenan, George, 71-72
Kennedy, John F., 71, 97, 104, 185
Kenya, Soviet informal penetration of, 64
Khrushchev, Nikita, 45-46, 66, 71, 95, 179, 185
Korea, United States civil action program, in, 85-86
Kuomintang, 53

Labor, role of, 27
Latin America, 18; Nazi economic warfare in, 41, 42, 43; United States informal penetration of, 69, 72, 78, 81-82, 94, 99-107; United States technical assistance to, 78
Laval, Pierre, 36, 113, 114
League for Israel-USSR Friendship Ties, 60
League of Nations, 141
Lebanon, American intervention in, 147, 187
Lenin, Nikolai, 31, 45, 46, 47, 49-50, 66, 134
Loyalty, psychology and sociology of, 116-38
Lumumba, Patrice, 148, 149

Magsaysay, President of the Philippines, 89
Mao Tse-tung, 46, 71, 130
Marshall Plan, 14, 56-57, 74, 84
Marx, Karl, 45, 48
Marxism, 45, 48
Marxist-Leninist theory, 45-48
Military, role of, 28
Military assistance programs, 14, 73
Military civil action programs, 85-87

Military training program, 83
Mola, General Emilio, 7
Monroe Doctrine, 192; Roosevelt corollary to, 192-93
Montevideo Conference (1933), 101
Munich Agreements, 40

Nasser, Gamal Abdel, 71, 125
Nationalism, 129-30
Nation-state, nature and functioning of, 168-72
Nation-state system, 4; informal penetration and, 156-176; conflict among nations, patterns of, 157-60; international organizations, role of, on world scene, 165-68, 173; international stability, 160-65; nation-state, nature and functioning of, 168-72; power in world politics, nature of, 156-57; nature and functioning of, 172-76
Nazi experience, informal attack, 30-44; Austria, 37-39; Czechoslovakia, 33-34, 39-41; economic warfare, 41-44; France, 34-37; South-West Africa, 34; Soviet experience compared with, 66-67
New nations: emergence of, 12, 14; problems of, 78; targets for informal penetration, 24-25
New York Times, The, 96-97
Non-governmental access, 17, 18
Non-intervention, doctrine of, 69, 101, 106-07, 177, 198; costs and benefits of, 188
North Atlantic Treaty Organization (NATO), 57, 80-81, 142, 187, 190, 194
Nuclear weapons, development of, 12

"Opex" program, 143
Organization for European Economic Cooperation (OEEC), 74-75
Organization of African Unity (OAU) 145-46
Organization of American States (OAS), 82, 101, 146-

OAS (*continued*)
147, 151

Organizations, international: informal access by, 17, 18, 24, 61-62, 140-55; United States, 81-83; role of, on world scene, 165-168, 173

Overseas Education Fund, National League of Women Voters, 90-91

Overt informal penetration, 10-11

Parti Populaire Francais, 37

Pcacc Corps, U.S., 79-80

Philippine Islands, United States political development program in, 89

Point IV program, 78, 84

Political development program, United States, 88-91

Power in world politics, nature of, 156-57

Pravda, 191

Prime-Presse, 36

Progressive Youth Circle, 60

Propaganda, 18, 43, 51, 61, 82, 115

"Protocols of the Elders of Zion, The," 30-31

Public Law 480, 78

Quasi-governmental access, 17, 18

Quisling, Vidkun, 113

Radio Free Europe, 82

Rauschning, Herman, 113

Rumania, 130, 189

Rumanian Iron Guard, 34

Rusk, Dean, 182, 187

Russian Revolution (1917), 51

Ruthenia, 41

Saturday Evening Post, 96

Schering, A. G., 41

Schuman, Robert, 76

Schuschnigg, Kurt von, 38

Seyss-Inquart, Arthur von, 38, 39, 113, 114

Slovakia, 41

Smith-Mundt Act (1948), 83

"Sources of Soviet Conduct, The" (Kennan), 71-72

South Vietnam, United States civil action program in, 87

South-West Africa, Nazi informal penetration of, 34

Soviet Union: experience in informal attack, 45-67; China, 53; cultural diplomacy, 62-64; Czechoslovakia, 50, 57-60; economic aid programs, 64-65; foreign policy, 65-66; front organizations, 60-62; Nazi experience compared with, 66-67; Spain, 53-54; technical assistance programs, 64-65; ideological split with China, 64; Nazi attack on, 55

Spain, Soviet intervention in, 53-54; interventions since WWII, chapt. VII

Spanish Civil War, 53-54

Spheres of influence, 178-81, 186; *see also* Intervention

Stability, international, 160-65

Stalin, Joseph, 21, 45, 46, 49, 51, 66, 71

State Department, U. S., 17, 99

Stauffenberg, Klaus von, 113, 114, 118, 124

Students, role of, 27

Subsidiaries, foreign, 19

Substantive accessibility, 21-23, 115

Sudeten Free Corps, 40

Sudeten German party, 39-40

Sudeten Germans, 33, 39-40

Sudetenland, Nazi take-over of, 39

Sun Yat-sen, 53

"Support," informal: concept of, 9, 15; Soviet, 64-65; United States, 73-78, 85-87

Technical accessibility, 21-23

Technical assistance programs, 14, 64-65, 78-79

Techniques of informal penetration, 6-7, 9-10, 23-24

Technology, informal penetration and, 10, 12

Tito, Marshal, 46, 55, 187

Togliatti, Italian Communist party leader, 57

Toguri, Eva (Tokyo Rose), 113, 135

Treason, *see* Disloyalty
"Trojan horse tactics," 7
Trotsky, Leon, 31
Truman, Harry S., 71, 73, 78
Tshombe, Moise, 149
Turkey: Soviet informal penetration of, 54; United States economic and military aid to, 73
"Twenty-one Demands," 51-52

United Arab Republic, 125; Soviet informal penetration of, 64
United Nations, 56, 69, 70, 82, 141, 142-45, 147-51, 153-55, 194; Congo operation, 148-50; development of code of intervention, 207
United Nations Economic Commission, 144-45
United Nations Educational, Scientific and Cultural Organization (UNESCO), 143
United Nations Expanded Technical Assistance Program, 144
United Nations Food and Agricultural Organization, 143
United Nations International Children's Emergency Fund (UNICEF), 143, 145, 152
United Nations Relief and Rehabilitation Administration (UNRRA), 73, 141
United Nations Relief and Works Agency for Palestine Refugees, 144
United Nations Special Committee on Palestine, 147
United Nations Special Fund, 144
United States, informal penetration by, 69-110; Alliance for Progress program, 99-107; covert operations, 91-99, 204; cultural exchange program, 80, 83-84; economic aid programs, 73-78, 87-89; foreign policy, 69-70; international organizations, 81-83; Latin America, 69, 72, 78, 81-82, 94, 99-107; military aid

U.S. (*continued*)
program, 73; military civil action programs, 85-87; military interventions since WWII, chapt. VII; North Atlantic Treaty Organization, 80-81; political development program, 88-91; technical assistance programs, 78-80, 199-200
United States Agency for International Development, 200
United States Central Intelligence Agency, 204
United States Information Agency, 17, 61, 82
Universal Postal Union, 143
U-2 spy plane incident, 94-95

Vlasov, General, 113, 114, 125
Voice of America program, 7

Warsau Pact, 183
Wars of Religion, 8
What is to Be Done? (Lenin), 49
Woman's International Democratic Federation, 61
World Center for the Struggle Against Jewry, 36
World Congress of Doctors, 62
World Council of Churches, 140
World Federation of Democratic Youth, 61
World Federation of Scientific Workers, 61
World Federation of Trade Workers, 62
World Health Organization, 143, 152
World Meteorological Organization, 143
World Peace Council, 61
World Veterans Federation, 140
World War II, 50, 55

Yemen, Soviet informal penetration of, 64
Young Men's Christian Association, 140
Yugoslav Communist party, 55
Yugoslavia, 55-56, 187

Zorin, Valerian, 58